OVERCOMING YOUR PERFECT STORM

How to stay afloat when life swamps your boat.

By
Douglas M. Clark

ISBN: 978-0999665015

Library of Congress Control Number: 2017903137

TABLE OF CONTENTS

Foreword 1

Introduction..3

Chapter 1..9

Learning to Sail:

The Power of Imperfection

Chapter 2...21

High Hope and Aspirations:

The Power of Hope!

Chapter 3...35

What's the Use:

The Power of Purpose!

Chapter 4...43

You Are What You Think:

The Power of Our Minds!

Chapter 5...59

Ouch:

The Power of Words!

Chapter 6...73

Lone Ranger:

The Power of Connection

Chapter 7 79

One Bad Apple:

The Power of Friends!

Chapter 8 91

Drinking Poison:

The Power of Forgiveness!

Chapter 9 103

Saying Thank You:

The Power of Gratitude!

Chapter 10 113

What Can I Do For You:

The Power of Generosity!

Chapter 11 129

Sedentary Malaise:

The Power of Exercise

Chapter 12 137

Spoil Yourself:

The Power of Self Care

Chapter 13 147

Button it up:

The Power of Silence

Chapter 14 155

Kicking and Screaming:

The Power of Perspective!

Chapter 15 165

Smooth Sailing:

The Power of Affirmation

Author Biography 169

FOREWORD

You will be glad you picked up Douglas M. Clark's Overcoming Your Perfect Storm. Whether you are currently experiencing a "perfect storm" of your own, or merely looking for tools to deal with such a storm should it arise in the future, you have found a wonderful resource.

It is an honor to know Doug and a joy to read his story which will touch so many. It was Doug's compassion that compelled him to write this book. His own experience of hopelessness and overwhelm eventually led to questioning everything he knew, resulting in growth and deepening of insight and wisdom. But that was not enough. His generous spirit required the candid sharing of his own journey through the darkness and into the light so that others could benefit as well.

Doug describes his struggles and abject despair. He suffered a series of profound losses socially, financially, physically, emotionally, and psychologically. After he lost so much of what mattered most to him, he had to rethink his entire life, including his closely held beliefs. He faced himself by fighting old patterns, gathering information, and pushing himself to grow. He eventually found his way out of the abyss. The result was a more perceptive and hopeful individual, but it had been a long and arduous road. In this compelling first person narrative, Doug outlines the steps he took to arrive at a place of peace and joy. Further, he incorporates research, knowledge and beliefs from the fields of mental health. neuroscience, physical science and spiritual studies in order to reach and assist the broadest base of those in need of emotional support and guidance.

Doug's storm was severe, but his desire to move forward led to a wealth of information. What he learned, and now shares with us, about growth and well-being is a lasting treasure.

Marcia Conley, MA, LPC

Psychotherapist, Counselor, Life Coach

Introduction

I'm sitting with coffee in hand, the warm sun gently kissing my face. The view of the fifteenth fairway of the golf course is incomparable.

I have been sharing a house, and the view that accompanies it, with a friend for the last several months. I will tell you more about how I got here later but let me start by saying it has been a long seven years.

Through a combination of economic loss, a relationship meltdown, physical maladies, personal crises, and both a mental and emotional breakdown, I have had the opportunity to go through a very introspective time. I call it my perfect storm.

Do I wish these things hadn't happened?

Yes and no.

The mental, emotional, spiritual, and physical pain were excruciating. Their presence was dark and ominous. I felt like I had to look up to see the bottom.

Is everything in my life perfect now?

Depends on how you measure it.

Finances are still tight but looking up. Personal relationships are a bit thin but improving. Mentally and emotionally, I'm probably still a bit fragile. Spiritually, I'm immature.

But I have learned so much about life and myself, and I am overwhelmed with that sense of well-being that happens when everything is in alignment. Or if that is too squishy for you—when everything is "firing on all cylinders."

Do I wish I could do some things over again?

Of course.

As Chester W. Nimitz has said, "Hindsight is notably cleverer than foresight." I have learned tons.

For much of the last seven years, I felt like I was in a deep abyss. And as I lay there, in that place, I spent time contemplating, studying, devouring truths about life. That fragile tenacity became crucial for me to overcome my perfect storm.

I realized that I was not alone. I realized that you were experiencing your perfect storm and that you needed help.

I recognized that was my life purpose to help you make it.

As I have shared my story, it has been my privilege to help others just like you make it through their storm. Showing them the steps that I took and giving them support as they walked through the tempest.

I think of Shelly. She found her husband was having multiple bi-sexual affairs and was abusing prescription drugs. She found herself rolled up in a ball on her bed, unable to move. Ready to give up. She remembered hearing me talk about my storm and the steps I took and with what felt to her as her last gasp of strength. I am happy to say that after walking through the steps in this book with her – she is a different person. Now she is a woman full of life, hope, vibrancy and energy.

Then there was Stuart who was wrongly accused of wrongdoing at this job. He felt his world was crashing in. he didn't know how he was going to continue. He too reached out and after implementing the steps that I present in this book successfully started a new chapter in his life.

There is also Joe (single) and Nancy (married) who were caught having an affair with each other. Their job had a 'morality clause' and they found themselves unemployed and Nancy facing an ugly divorce. After implementing the steps presented in this book, I am happy to say they have risen from the ashes of their mistake and are looking with confidence to their future.

In the following pages you will learn about

The Power of Imperfection

The Power of Hope

The Power of Purpose

The Power of Our Minds

The Power of Words

The Power of Connection

The Power of Friends

The Power of Forgiveness

The Power of Gratitude

The Power of Generosity

The Power of Exercise

The Power of Self Care

The Power of Silence

The Power of Perspective

The Power of Affirmation

You too can make it through your storm. Implementing these truths will help you weather any storm that blows your way.

So, read on. Learn. Put into practice. Let my story help you.

I am not afraid of storms
for I am learning
how to sail my ship.
Louisa May Alcott

CHAPTER 1

Learning to Sail:
The Power of Imperfection

Life.

It seems like one moment we're gleefully playing in the grand sandbox of life when, all of a sudden, a bully comes out of nowhere and kicks sand in our face.

For some of us, the innocent, gleeful playtime ends at an early age, maybe three or four years old. For others, it's when we reach our teen years, while for others, it's in our twenties or thirties.

The sand may be the loss of someone close, verbal or physical abuse, a sudden illness, or an injury. Maybe it's just the wear and tear of life. Some are lucky enough to still be dreaming at midlife. But the truth is, at some point, we're pushed through circumstances, so we ask, "Am I enjoying this thing called life?"

Please don't get me wrong. Life isn't a negative. Life is a positive. It just seems that the events of life keep slapping us around, and before we know it, the innocent gleeful outlook we had early in life is replaced with worry and fear.

It's common for professional golfers to experience this. After thousands of rounds of golf, a professional golfer can begin missing putts that he used to make with ease. He can even develop what's referred to as the yips, which are involuntary muscle spasms making putting very difficult.

A pro golfer can start missing putts because it's a human tendency to remember our misses instead of our makes. With time, the missed putts start adding up and weigh on the golfer's mind to such a degree that he has a hard time remembering his successful putts. He begins to feel like he's a failure and thus looks at his future putts as insurmountable challenges.

But does life have to feel that way? Do we have to lose that sense of wonder? That curiosity? That positive outlook? Do we have to get the yips? I don't believe so.

I recently began experiencing the results of choices (both mine and others) and the effects of my genetics (both good and bad), and I definitely wasn't enjoying the moment. Quite honestly, I wasn't enjoying life at all. I call it my perfect storm!

Using the metrics common to most, I was on top of the world, with high hopes and aspirations. I had a beautiful family. I was bringing in a great income. I had a net worth with plenty of zeros. I was a respected leader in my community. I was serving as a state representative, a position I felt honored to hold.

That's when the big wave hit. Actually, it was more than a wave. It was one gigantic storm with a series of tsunami-sized waves. It didn't hit all at once, and as I write this, I can still feel the effects.

I remember when the wave hit like it was yesterday. I was halfway through my term as a representative in the Arizona state legislature when the economy went sour. At that time, I was making a six-figure income in real estate, and with the crash, the whole industry went south, along with my income and most of my holdings.

Suddenly, my family's biggest concern wasn't where we were vacationing next summer but rather how we were going to pay the mortgage.

We fell behind on our bills. We lost our house. We filed for bankruptcy. I thought that was the end of the storm. I was wrong.

We lived in a small town. The church we attended experienced an ugly split. Of course, I must ask, is there ever a pretty one?

I was unaware of any discord as I rode my scooter past the church one afternoon and heard a voice in my head say, "*The pastor's in trouble!* ". Immediately, I pulled over and called him up. "Are you okay?" I asked.

His response scared me; "Doug, I don't think I'm going to make it."

"Is there someone with you right now?" I asked.

He said yes then went on to explain that he had been accused of embezzling from the church coffers. I heard myself say, "I'm here for you. I'll come beside you and support you through this." I committed to walking with him through this dark moment in his life and that of his church.

What a shock it was when, because of my willingness to assist, people started questioning my integrity. Did I mention that I lived in a small town?

When your integrity is questioned, you really have a hard time leading. In short order, the half-dozen or so positions of leadership that I had in the community melted away. Among them: high school soccer coach—gone, as parents yelled obscenities from the stands; president of the arts council—gone, as a board member called for a vote of confidence and the majority agreed; and president of the chamber of commerce—gone, as the founder's wife was the one who started the terrible rumor about the pastor.

I was left wondering when the waves would settle down. Maybe now? No, not yet.

Did all this just coincidently happen at once? Possibly. Were they coordinated and related? Also possible.

At the same time, the cracks in my marriage grew into canyons. After twenty-five years of marriage, my wife and I parted ways. The heartache was terrible.

Could the waves get worse? Surely not!

Yes, they could, and they did.

While all this was happening, I experienced a myriad of health issues leading to four surgeries. The most severe of these was a recurrence of diverticulitis. Without going into details, just know it's a very painful intestinal disorder that, if left untreated, can lead to death.

I fought it (valiantly or foolishly, who knows) until, finally, I knew it had the upper hand, and I surrendered to the surgeon's knife.

Surely, I had hit bottom, right? Surely, the waves had to start leveling off.

Well, not so quickly.

Meanwhile, back at the church offices, it was found that the accusations against the pastor were completely false. In fact, wisely or foolishly, the pastor had been putting the church's electricity bill on his credit card in the hope that the church's finances would turn around. As a result, he had sabotaged his own financial position.

After three long years of trying to get things back on track, we decided that the best course of action was to close its doors. What a painful process. I still remember the last day, locking the doors after everyone had left.

During those three years, it had been my responsibility to oversee the daily operations of the church and facilities. Monday through Friday, a school used our facilities. I had spent evenings coordinating the use of the facilities by various community groups. Saturdays were set aside to make sure that everything was ready for weekend services.

This was in addition to running my consulting business.

On Sundays, I would arrive early and make sure everything was ready for the day and welcome each volunteer as they arrived to serve. I would then spend the day making sure that everyone felt welcomed and that everything ran as smoothly as possible.

This responsibility gave me purpose and an opportunity to connect. I didn't realize how important this thread was in my emotional, mental, and spiritual well-being.

With the closing of those doors came the end of an opportunity to connect weekly with fellow attendees, volunteers, and leaders. The diaspora began. Everyone scurried to find a new connecting place. Some even moved out of town.

Now that they were gone, I suddenly realized how important a role these people had played in my life. They had become my friends, my support system. The extreme sense of loss that I felt surprised me.

Surely, that was the end of the storm.

Well, not quite yet.

As all this was going on, I started experiencing severe bouts of depression. At first, I really didn't know what was going on. I just called it the blues. I was unmotivated and listless. I questioned the purpose of my existence.

My chest was heavy. I felt like I couldn't inhale, like I couldn't breathe. I couldn't live.

After a while, I realized that it was much more than just the blues. One day, I found myself on the corner of a street in downtown Phoenix sobbing uncontrollably. I couldn't help it. And I didn't care that people were staring.

In a dark corner of my mind, I knew that I needed to get help, or I wasn't going to make it. I was cracking.

Friends used to call me the Energizer Bunny, but now my battery was depleted of energy. I found that I was emotionally, mentally, physically, and spiritually bankrupt. I felt fatigued. I felt shame and was embarrassed to find myself in this state. "I'm a guy!", I thought, "Guys are strong—we don't crack. We don't need help."

Standing there on the street, my brain was lost in a fog. My limbs were as heavy as logs. My fingers? Immovable stubs. My emotions were like delicate eggshells smashed beneath the weight of my circumstances.

But somehow, I also knew that if I didn't pull out my phone right at that moment and make myself accountable in the form of an appointment, I would back out.

I asked Siri for counselors in my area. A list came up on my screen, so I chose one and sent an e-mail. In the e-mail, I admitted that I was desperate and needed help. The counselor responded and quickly adjusted her schedule to accommodate me.

Fortunately, she was fantastic. What a relief. Within a couple of sessions, I felt so much better. I was making headway.

But counseling is expensive, and because I was still in a very tight place financially, I quit going. In my mind, I hoped that I'd turned the corner, although I knew my handle on life was tenuous at best.

About that time, I experienced Robin Williams' suicide. I say *experienced* because when you're barely hanging on, you feel it when someone else gives up.

Tragically, at the same time, a friend of mine also called it quits. Family members found him lifeless at his home.

So, as I sat in a coffee shop in Fort Worth, Texas, I broadcast via my blog what I was wrestling with. I called it "Coming Out of the Closet!"

I too wanted to quit. Jump off this ride called life. Get out. Stop the pain. Man it was hard, admitting that I didn't have it together. There seems to be a special weight on us males to be strong, and self-assured. Maybe self-imposed at times, but one reinforced by our culture.

I felt that I was somehow handing in my man card by admitting that I was fragile.

At that time there really were only two people who had an inkling of what I was experiencing. With them, I would often struggle to speak a full sentence without falling apart into a blubbering mess. But with everyone else, I would put on my game face and act like all was okay.

But hey, now the good news! I'm better now!

Oh, believe me, I'm not perfect. But then, despite what I used to believe about myself, I never was. When I was young I used to say, "I thought I made a mistake once, but I was wrong!"

Deep down I kind of believed that. I felt that I could do no wrong. I was always right. *My* perspective was the correct one. *My* actions were above reproach. In short, I was perfect.

And so, when I was slapped with the realization that I wasn't perfect, what I really needed to know was that that was okay.

I began to learn one of my biggest lessons: I am imperfect, and there is no shame in that.

For me, the best way to show that I accepted that fact was by asking for help. From my counselor, my pastor, my family, and selected peers. In my mind I played the scenario out with each one – I convinced myself that they would judge me and agree with me that I was a complete failure unworthy and incapable of rehabilitation!

A funny thing happened—none of that happened. They were there for me!

The shame that I was sure I would experience and the certainty of their rejection never happened.

Instead, I experienced the warm embrace of their acceptance, assistance, healing, and encouragement. And this became the foundation upon which I could begin to rebuild the new Doug.

As you find yourself in your perfect storm and your lifeboat is becoming swamped with the force of the wind and waves. You feel like you are about to go under, and one of your greatest fears is that people will realize that the life that you had so perfectly planned and presented to the world isn't so perfect after all.

Like me, you aren't perfect either!

Deep down inside of you, you already know it. Admitting it is the difficult part—mainly because we aren't sure what our friends will say when they find out.

But guess what? They already know!

So, embrace it. Accept it. The sooner we embrace our imperfections and release the shame that we have stuffed inside, the sooner we can actually inhale, breathe, and live! Once we do that, with confidence we each can declare that we are not afraid of storms, for we are learning how to sail our ships.

I encourage you to reach out and pick a person to confide in. Call them.

Get professional help. Call a Counselor.

Call your pastor.

Hope is the thing with feathers

That perches in the soul

And sings the tune without the words

And never stops

at all.

Emily Dickinson

CHAPTER 2

High Hope and Aspirations:
The Power of Hope!

I want to be a fireman!

I want to be a doctor!

I want to be an astronaut!

I want to be a teacher!

I want to be president!

Remember those declarations you made as a young kid?

Our aspirations had no limit. We could dream as high as the sky. We begin life with high hopes and aspirations!

The other day, I was looking at a photo mural of my boys that hangs on my wall. The pictures show them when they were young: from newborn to probably about five years old.

Playing in the sand.

Holding their Certificates of Merit.

Standing by Mickey Mouse.

They are grown now; fine young men that any father could easily be proud of. But as I gazed at the pictures I was struck by the sparkle in their eyes.

Their faces showed complete wonderment and trust. You could tell that they expected nothing but good to come into their lives.

I suddenly found myself contrasting those faces with what the faces of grown adults, captured in pictures, generally look like. Yes, maybe one of you or me.

Rarely is it the same.

I'm not talking about size, shape, and age difference. I am talking about essence; we stage a smile and tilt our head. We try to show that we are genuinely happy about the moment.

But there is this other aspect.

A shadow of doubt. A touch of hurt. A glint of disappointment. A touch of anger or wistfulness.

All of these are displayed via "worry" wrinkles, or a frown line or a downturn at the corner of the mouth. Maybe sadness in the eyes.

What happened?

How can humans begin their lives with complete delight during early childhood, only to become skeptical and guarded adults?

Life. That's what happens.

Author and researcher Dr. Martin Seligman has done extensive research on optimism, happiness, and meaning. He spent a couple decades studying optimism's opposite: helplessness.

He refers to a study that was done with two dogs. Both dogs were given shocks at random intervals. One could press a lever to stop the shocks. The other could not.

The first dog quickly discovered how to stop the shocks, and immediately began enjoying life again— playing, sleeping, and eating. The other dog, the one who couldn't do anything about the shocks, eventually succumbed to their continual onslaught and his discomfort. He gave up, curling into a helpless little ball in the corner as the shocks continued.

That was part one of the study.

Part two went like this: the same two dogs were put into a new environment. This time, both dogs were given the means to easily avoid the shocks.

The first dog, who had originally found the solution to the shocks, quickly discovered what it took to stop them again. The other dog, however, gave up without trying—curling into a ball as the shocks continued (and continued and continued). This dog surrendered to the situation, even though he now had the power to change his situation. This dog had learned helplessness.

So have we.

After being shocked so many times throughout our lives, too often we learn helplessness and just give up.

What can we do about it?

Experts agree that there is one huge thing that we can do to regain our optimism, which feeds our hope.

One of the best ways to do this is to be committed to something larger than just our own lives.

Most who know me see me as an extrovert. Outgoing, I love to be in public. I'm not afraid to be in front. And, while that is true, in my personal life I am very private, preferring to keep my feelings inside and discounting my needs. And with all that had recently transpired in my life, I had become even more withdrawn.

Yes, when needed, I could call on my extroverted superpowers and be the personable, "party-in-a-box," energetic, go-to guy. But it took everything I had.

I found myself avoiding scenarios where I would have to interact. As I did, my helplessness escalated to hopelessness.

But then I stumbled upon Victor Frankl's book *Man's Search for Meaning*. Frankl was an Austrian psychiatrist who was imprisoned at Auschwitz and several other concentration camps for three years during the Second World War.

During his internment, he observed people both survive and succumb to the horrendous circumstances and treatment that was the norm in the concentration camps. What puzzled Victor was why—when given the same meager amount of food, lack of hygiene, minimal sleep, deplorable living conditions, and mistreatment— did some survive while others gave up?

In short, he concluded that the prisoners who gave up did so because they had lost hope. They couldn't see that anything would ever change, and so they gave up. They couldn't believe that their current existence had any meaning.

I can't even begin to fathom the suffering that those prisoners went through. They did nothing to deserve their punishment. They were stripped of resources to survive even a single day and had no reason to believe that anything would change for the better.

This is where I found myself.

I was in my own self-created emotional, mental, and spiritual concentration camp, and I couldn't see that anything would change.

I had lost my hope.

Frankl declared in his book that "happiness couldn't be pursued, it must ensue. It is the unintended side effect of one's personal dedication to a cause greater than oneself or as the by-product of one's surrender to a person other than oneself."

He believed that when we connect with and commit to others, helplessness cannot escalate to hopelessness.

When we connect and commit with others, hope is fostered.

After I read Frankl's book, I decided I needed to change my course of action. Instead of withdrawing from everything and everyone, I realized I needed to connect and engage.

So, I chose to take some concrete, measurable steps.

First, I told God how I felt. I yelled at him. I swore at him. I told him it wasn't fair. I had me a good ol' pity party.

I did what I call the "Nancy Kerrigan."

Let me explain.

Nancy Kerrigan was a professional ice skater. In 1994, she was assaulted by a couple of guys, at the behest of competitor Tonya Harding, who bashed her legs with a metal bar in hope that she would no longer be able to compete in the Olympic Games, thereby guaranteeing Harding placement on the American team.

A video captured the moment when Kerrigan was on the ground, writhing in pain and crying out, "Why? Why? Why me?"

I did that with God. "Why? Why? Why me?"

My *why* was a victim's cry. I felt I had been wronged. What was happening to me wasn't fair. But, at least, directing words to God was a start.

After I was done with my heavenward pleadings, I started reaching out to others. This was step number two. I called up two men who in the past had reached out to me in friendship and invited them to join me for coffee. They both accepted.

The three of us spent twenty minutes together, a time that, because of its brevity, could seem meaningless and insignificant.

But I knew it was more than that!

As we sipped our coffee, we just talked about small meaningless stuff. And although I did not give them a glimpse of what was going on, I benefited. It was rich. We were sharing life. Connecting, not isolating.

I have no idea if the moments we shared were life-changing to them at all—but they certainly were to me. I began inviting people to eat a meal with me, and I accepted any invitation to dine with others.

Next, I joined a hiking group and started going hiking with them at least once a week. It was a perfect activity for me. I love to be active, and I needed to be with others!

But I wasn't ready to bare my soul with strangers.

I found in this group that I could retain a certain amount of anonymity.

Usually, the people around me were busy being chatterboxes, and I didn't have to say a thing. For most of the members of the group, it seemed, the hike was their opportunity to distribute their daily allotment of 30,000 words spoken.

If someone did toss conversation my way, all I had to do was ask a question, and they jumped headlong into an expansive answer.

And because of the nature the trails we hiked, we would often be forced to walk single file. This, in turn, naturally put the brakes on any following conversation; there was never a chance for me to join in.

The conversation would begin all over again with the next person who needed to fulfill their daily quota of words.

I also intentionally scheduled a weekly golf outing with my golf partner. We had golfed many times in the past—but now my invitations were intentional. Not for the improvement of my game, but to connect with someone I could trust.

Church became a weekly activity. Surprisingly, this was the toughest one. I love being the church. Meaning, I love to give. I love to be kind. I love to forgive. I love to help and encourage others. But I hate going to church.

I've been to church more than any single person should have to go. You see, I grew up in Latin America, where my family served as missionaries. One of our responsibilities was to go to churches and encourage the pastors and parishioners.

At one point during my teenage years, I was going to church more than five times a week. A friend told me that I would have made a great Catholic!

On top of that, as an adult, I have been involved in church leadership for more than twenty-five years. Because I have this perspective from the inside, I have unfortunately allowed myself to become hypercritical if something is done incorrectly or unnecessarily or distastefully in the church service.

As I previously mentioned, my home church had just gone through a horrible split. False accusations made by church members ripped lives, friendships, trust, and community to shreds. I was part of the group that helped gather the church's broken pieces. We tried to work to a semblance of wholeness before ultimately closing the doors a couple of years later.

It was a heart-wrenching experience, and I didn't want to expose that tender spot, but it dawned on me that I just needed to get over it. So, I began sneaking into the least conspicuous, back-of-the-back-row kind of seat in a neighborhood church located right across the street from where I was living.

Fortunately, they weren't an incredibly warm or welcoming group; I could sneak in and out without anyone seeming to care.

The last change I made in my quest for connection was to volunteer at a nonprofit. I gave them eight hours of my time every week. Up to this point, I had made a living as a consultant for nonprofits. Forming executive boards, developing bylaws and articles of Incorporation. Creating vision statements, balancing budgets, and resolving organizational issues.

However, I didn't tell this nonprofit what I did for a living. They put me in charge of folding letters and stuffing envelopes. Yep, here was ex-millionaire, ex-state representative, ex-whatever, in the basement folding mailers.

I loved it!

The staff members that I served were some of the sweetest, most giving, dedicated, and passionate people that I've ever met.

Did sealing stacks of envelopes help?

Yes!

Did my eating and golfing and hiking efforts help?

Yes!

Did my efforts to re-engage at church help?

Yes!

As I continued to connect with God, I soon experienced a heart-shift. And instead of asking, *why me?* in a whiny, this-isn't-fair tone of voice, I started humbly asking, *Why? What can I learn from this?*

My dinners and coffee time with friends became something I looked forward to. No agenda. No bullet points to cover. Just relationship. My other efforts were gaining traction too.

Hiking was something that I had always enjoyed, but I will admit the snail's pace that most people hiked bugged me horribly. And the 'Chatty Cathyies' drove me insane. But I found comfort, acceptance, and camaraderie with the group as we hiked the dusty desert mountains surrounding Phoenix.

I've always called golf my "therapy." There is something about stepping onto the tee box and smelling the fresh-cut grass and water. Viewing the beautifully manicured fairways and greens. Stepping into the soft sand in the sand traps. Watching the wildlife—the coyotes, groundhogs, snakes, and birds chirping in the trees. All capped off by the bright-blue sky and cotton-ball clouds floating above.

Now, experiencing my golf therapy sessions with someone I could trust, boosted my confidence. I slowly let my friend, my golf buddy, know what was going on inside of me. His acceptance, empathy, and compassion allowed the sanctuary of the golf course, coupled with his friendship, to be truly healing therapy.

Back at my neighborhood church, I rarely made it through the whole service at first. For many months, I would walk out (in a respectful manner) before the service came to a conclusion. Regularly, I would quietly weep in my seat when something was said or done that touched me deeply.

After about six months, I found that I could actually make it through an entire church service. I even began telling people, "You know, I think I am kind of falling in love with this little church that I've been going to!"

I began to look forward to touching base weekly with some of the people I had met there. I began to wonder whether, maybe, they weren't initially friendly because intuitively they could sense I really didn't want to be there—and that I really wasn't ready for relationship.

At the nonprofit where I volunteered, I started bringing in cookies, frozen yogurt, whatever I could think up, just so we could interact and get to know each other better.

Wow, these people had hearts of gold. They were so precious and giving. Toiling for subpar wages so that less-fortunate people around the world could eat. And although I never told them my story, they became a source of inspiration and grounding for me.

Like me, do you find yourself in a mental, spiritual and emotional concentration camp?

Can I gently, lovingly, humbly, boldly invite you to find something larger than yourself to live for, people you can connect with?

Can I suggest a short list of ways you can start connecting today?

- God: Ask Him why. He's a big boy. He can handle your questions. Your doubts. Your insults. Your insinuations. Your victim mentality.

- Friendships: Maybe start with those who have been reaching out to you. And then find activities and times where you can include others.

- Food: If you find yourself dining by yourself, invite someone to join you.

- Fun: If you find yourself watching television alone at night, invite someone to see a movie with you.

- Outreach: Maybe a social club or a Meet-Up. There are thousands of groups with thousands of people just like you who timidly want to belong. Or consider joining a church. Just be ready; they are as imperfect as you.

- Purpose: Volunteer at a nonprofit; catch their generous attitudes as they seek to help those who are more unfortunate than them.

It is crucial for us to discover the meaning of our existence, even in the most brutal of moments, and thus, find hope.

I promise you that, as you do these things, you will experience a shift. You will start moving from helpless to hopeful.

The purpose of life is a life of purpose.

Robert Byrne

CHAPTER 3

What's the Use:
The Power of Purpose!

It seems that there are specific times in life when we seem more susceptible to thoughts of unworthiness and uselessness.

The first is graduating from high school, when you are told "The world is your oyster!"—and you suddenly realize that you have never been taught how to crack the shell.

The second is seven years into marriage, when you feel the magnitude of raising kids, and the daunting task of providing for your family slaps you silly. Some call this the seven-year itch.

Next is the proverbial 'mid-life crisis'. That is when begin asking ourselves if this is all there is to life, and we go out and purchase a beautiful sports car.

The fourth time arrives when you retire and find there is nothing to motivate you to get out of bed in the morning.

Of all these, the last—retirement—is probably the biggest black hole. Our society sells retirement as some sort of end-of-life goal, our final great achievement.

We have swallowed the lie that when one hits sixty-seven the best thing a person can do is retire.

We live our whole lives aiming for that golden age when we don't have to work anymore.

Interestingly, after the retirement party, many people become apathetic, ill, and are soon six feet under.

Why is that?

It's called the "Retirement Effect."

According to researcher and author Dan Buettner, the two most vulnerable times in a person's life are the first twelve months after birth and the year following retirement.

You have probably heard stories about perfectly healthy individuals who died shortly after they retired from a lifelong career.

Some researchers suspect that, for these people, the end of their career also signified the end of their purpose in life, which affected their health and well-being.

A study of retired employees of Shell Oil found that men and women who retired early (age fifty-five) were more likely to die earlier than those who retired at age sixty-five.

A similar study of almost 17,000 healthy Greeks showed that the risk of death increased by 51percent after retirement.

These two studies suggest that there may be some risk involved in defining self by one's career.

It seems important to reshape life's big questions and find ways to continue serving a purpose, even after retirement, to improve chances of a longer, healthier life.

Tucked in just before the Retirement Effect is another period where a person—generally a male in his late forties to early fifties—starts wondering if this is all there is to life. He goes out and buys a sports car to get that adrenaline rush again. It is jokingly called a midlife crisis. But there is nothing funny about it.

And this is where I found myself.

As I look back, I now recognize that I—actively—participated in creating the dilemma in which I found myself.

About eight years prior to this, I started saying, out loud to friends and family, "I have lived a full life. I've had more great life experiences than I deserve. I would be okay if I died now."

What in the world?

By speaking those statements, I really was admitting that I no longer had a reason to exist. And as the challenges of life began piling up, I had no dream, no passion, nothing I was committed to that was bigger than me.

I had no purpose.

One of the common features among people who live with purpose is their ability to find meaning in the things that happen to them.

In essence, purpose-driven people know how to turn life's lemons into delicious lemonade.

Because I had lost sight of my purpose, my lemonade factory was not functioning well. The lemons were stacking up and starting to sour.

I needed to find my purpose.

Science has confirmed the healthy benefits of having purpose. Having a strong sense of purpose can help you

- live longer;
- protect yourself against heart disease;
- prevent Alzheimer's disease;
- better handle pain;
- experience more satisfying relationships; and
- better handle life's difficulties.

Purpose can offer a psychological buffer against obstacles. Thus, a person with a strong sense of purpose remains satisfied with life, even while experiencing a difficult day.

At an early age she was fascinated by stories of people who lived their lives in service to others.

At the age of 18 she left home to become a nun and after teaching for 20 years she felt led to leave the convent and help the poor while living among them.

The first year was incredibly difficult. With no income, she begged for food and supplies and experienced doubt, loneliness, and temptation to return to the comfort of convent life.

Almost 50 years later, at 76 years of age she was leading a movement had grown to include 4,000 other ladies (sisters) and 300 men who had committed to the same mission as herself: managing orphanages, AIDS hospices, and charity centers around the world.

Caring for refugees, the blind, disabled, aged, alcoholics, the poor and homeless and victims of floods, epidemics, and famine. Operating 610 missions in 123 countries.

Purpose of living life for others gave her life. Maybe we should take a page from those do-gooders, the Mother Teresa-types in our lives.

They might be better off in the long run than those who seek joy from more shallow pursuits.

Here is why: the gene that fights inflammation in a person's body and the gene that fights viruses and antibodies is strong among people who find joy from having a greater purpose in life.

Conversely, people who find joy only in pleasing themselves have higher incidents of inflammation and are more susceptible to viruses and antibodies.

"Doing good and feeling good have very different effects on the human genome, even though they generate similar levels of positive emotion," says researcher Steven Cole, a professor of medicine at the University of California, Los Angeles and a member of the university's Cousins Center for Psychoneuroimmunology.

He continued, "Apparently, the human genome is much more sensitive to different ways of achieving happiness than our conscious minds."

Could this be why we have heard it said, "It is better to give than to receive?"

Doing something meaningful and helpful brings emotional and psychological benefits to your life. It brings health, it brings life, it gets you up in the morning!

The key is to recognize that as long as we draw breath, we have purpose.

I recognize that I—still—have purpose, and I am going to live purposefully. Because of that, I am excited about today, tomorrow, and next week!

I've adopted the mantra, "I choose to make the **rest** of my life, the **best** of my life!"

Join me, won't you? Find something bigger than yourself that you can give yourself to. Find your purpose. It will keep you alive – quite literally!

Avoid stinkin' thinkin'.

Zig Ziglar

Finally, brothers, whatever is true, whatever is noble, whatever is right, whatever is pure, whatever is lovely, whatever is admirable if anything is excellent or praiseworthy—think about such things.

Apostle Paul

Chapter 4

You Are What You Think:
The Power of Our Minds!

As I sat in the doctor's (psychiatrist) office, I wondered what the prognosis was. I had come in because I was not well. Something wasn't right.

I could just tell.

I had been feeling depressed, sad, empty, and tearful. I no longer found interest or pleasure in activities that I used to find enjoyable. I wanted to sleep all the time. I seemed to get agitated easily. Mentally, I've always been a quick processor, but now it seemed like everything moved in slow motion; I couldn't concentrate and was having difficulty making decisions. I had no energy and was fatigued all the time. I also had strong feelings of worthlessness and guilt for no reason. Lastly, I had begun hoping I would die, and I even contemplated committing suicide.

But I needed an expert to diagnose and help treat whatever it was that I was experiencing.

I sat rigidly in my seat. Tense. My hands tightly grabbed the chair's armrest, ready to bolt. I was prepared for the worst, or so I thought.

"Well," the doctor declared, "you are definitely dealing with some challenging issues." His words hit me like a sledgehammer. "You are showing symptoms that we generally associate with individuals who suffer from a mental illness that we call Bipolar II." Then he added, kind of like the cherry on top, "And it also looks like you may be dealing with a degree of Obsessive Compulsive Personality Disorder. However," he continued, "You don't fit the typical Bipolar II profile. I believe you have just endured a tremendous amount of upheaval, and your mind is responding in this way."

He handed me a prescription and a sheet of paper with a number of book titles and websites, scheduled a follow up appointment, and sent me on my way. I walked out of his office in a fog.

What the heck?

What is Bipolar II?

What is Obsessive Compulsive Personality Disorder?

Now I knew everything, yet I knew nothing at all.

We throw the phrase, "I think he (or she) is bipolar," around a lot. In fact, a week later, I was lunching with a friend when she described an acquaintance as "bipolar." But how many people really know what that means?

It is amazing how we respond differently to physical illness than to mental illness. As a culture, we look down on those who suffer from mental illness. When someone is mentally ill, we tend to look down our nose at them and critically wonder why they can't keep it together. Or, we stay away because we are afraid that the suffering person is going to somehow do us harm.

Conversely, if we hear someone has cancer, we immediately want to draw that person to us and help. We feel bad for them, show them empathy and say how unfair it is that they are being afflicted that way.

Why is it so hard to embrace and empathize with someone who is suffering mentally?

It is for this reason that I had to really think long and hard about sharing this episode of my life.

Ultimately, I decided that, although I wasn't diagnosed with a Bipolar II, maybe my experience could assist in creating a shift in how we perceive mental illness. And maybe my story could give courage to another who was suffering.

After that initial visit with the doctor, I returned weekly so that he could monitor and assess my well-being. We would interact and share resources that we had been reading and what we had discovered about mental health. I would talk about the practices and habits I was implementing.

I also began seeing the counselor again whom I had reached out to originally. She was a godsend. She pushed back against our culture's need to label people suffering with mental issues. Her insights and reassurances assisted me greatly. She agreed with the doctor's assessment that I didn't fit the typical profile for Bipolar II and refused to put that label on me.

Nevertheless, because of my proximity to it and the reaction our culture has to it, I spent hours researching mental health and bipolar affliction in particular.

As far as the OCD diagnosis, I'm pretty sure the doctor came to that conclusion in part because of the five pages of double-spaced notes I had prepared in anticipation of my appointment with him.

However, I'm not going to unwrap that yet because I'm still getting everything in order! Get it? That was a joke!

But on the serious side, I really do like things in order. There are times when the need to have everything in order seems too overwhelming to me. I am learning that it is okay that my clothes hangers are not color coordinated and exactly one inch apart.

I found some comfort in the doctor's assessment of my condition; it at least explained—and validated—what I was experiencing.

But I still found myself yelling at the top of my voice in my car, as the voice on the audio book he'd recommended was telling me to "embrace my story."

"I don't like my story!" I screamed. "I don't like where I find myself, and I don't know how I got here!"

What happens when you don't like your story?

What happens when things that are out of your control impact you, potentially for the rest of your life, in a negative way?

Remember the study Dr. Martin Seligman performed with two dogs back in chapter 2? We read how one of the dogs found the secret lever and stopped the shocks, while the other curled up in a helpless little ball in the corner while the shocks continued.

The state of hopelessness.

What a terrible place to be.

Please realize that choosing to curl up in the corner (or in bed) as we helplessly let life shock us again and again is *the* quickest way to ensure we stay depressed and, in the process, destroy our psychological and immunological health.

There are simple yet powerful levers we can press that can assist us—and changes we can make—so we enjoy life and enjoy getting old!

Not long ago, it was my privilege to be the guest speaker to a group of people fifty-five years of age and above. As I shared this truth, most looked at me like I was delusional!

They were probably thinking, *What does this young whippersnapper know about aches, pains, disappointments, lack, failure?*

But a couple of them had a sparkle in their eye. They understood. They got it. They were enjoying getting old. By the end of the presentation, a few more had begun to believe that maybe, just maybe, they too could enjoy getting old.

When we feel helpless, it is because we have lost hope.

Hope is a powerful thing!

We talked about it briefly in an earlier chapter, but let's dig deeper.

Matt Biondi was one the greatest swimmers of all time (before Michael Phelps took center stage) and one of the most victorious Olympians of all time. He also happened to be a subject in Dr. Seligman's research.

During the 1998 Seoul Olympics, Biondi was expected to bring home gold in all seven of his events. His first two events were a disappointment (in his eyes); he received bronze and silver.

Dr. Seligman, a leading authority in the fields of positive psychology, resilience, learned helplessness, depression, and optimism and pessimism, sat watching the events at his home, listening to the announcers ponder whether Biondi would rebound following his two disappointments. "I sat in my living room, confident he would," writes Seligman in his book *Learned Optimism*.

How could he say that?

Why was he confident?

In Dr. Seligman's words, Biondi would bounce back "because his explanatory style was highly optimistic and he had shown us that he got faster—not slower—after defeat."

Maybe I should take a moment to make sure that we see the benefits of being optimistic. I don't want to assume that we are all on the same page. Some people seem to revel in being depressed and wallowing in what I call their "blueness."

Author Jessica Cassity presents ten reasons to be an optimist. All of them are supported through scientific research.

- When you are optimistic you *feel* healthier.
- When you are optimistic you *are* healthier.
- An optimist lives longer.
- An optimist is sick less.
- An optimist can better handle stress.
- For those of you looking for a companion, an optimist is the "best date."
- An optimist finds his or her job more fulfilling.
- An optimist receives more job offers and promotions.
- An optimist is better at bouncing back.

So now we know the value of being optimistic, we ask ourselves:

How can I become optimistic?

How can I get better after I do badly?

How can I restore that incredible, intangible, fantastic, life-giving thing called hope?

We can *learn* to be optimistic.

Yep, you can do that.

Don't believe it? Just stay with me and let me explain!

Experts used to believe that everything was a result of how we were created. Another way of saying it is, "We are who we are, and we can't change a thing!"

However, it is now understood that a person can adopt new cognitive strategies, which in turn result in different behaviors.

It is called Cognitive Behavioral Therapy.

This is not to be confused with "positive thinking!" Learning to be optimistic is not just implementing the power of thinking positively.

We all know that optimists see the glass as half full while pessimists see it as half empty. It is now understood—even if not experienced by us—that pessimists can learn to be optimists.

In the same way that you were once full of hope as a child, you can become hopeful again.

However, it is more than just saying positive things or singing happy songs. Don't get me wrong—those are good practices. But it is more than that.

You can return to hopefulness by learning a new set of cognitive skills. In other words, it boils down to *how* you interpret something that happens to you. *How* you think about a positive or negative event determines quite a bit.

Just like the dogs in Dr. Seligman's study, we as humans learn helplessness when we believe that nothing we do will change our circumstances, and in turn we give up.

So, what is the solution?

We need to change how we explain things to ourselves.

Do you know what I mean by that?

We have learned to be helpless by explaining to ourselves every time something "bad" happens that life is bad. If we are optimistic in how we explain life events to ourselves, it stops helplessness. If we are pessimistic, then we encourage helplessness.

Have you ever realized that you are always talking to yourself? There's a constant dialogue going on inside your head. Don't worry, that is normal!

When "bad" things happen to you, like getting laid off or arguing with a friend, what do you say to yourself in your internal dialogue?

A helpless person will think things like the following:

- It's my fault.
- It's going to last forever.

- It's going to jeopardize everything from now on.
- I can't expect anything better.

In contrast, a hopeful, optimistic person will think things like the following:

- I couldn't do anything about the outcome.
- It's only temporary.
- It's part of life.
- I can do better next time.

The way that you interpret events in your life dictates your level of hopefulness.

Marci Schimoff explains it this way in her book, *Happy for No Reason*:

Our minds—made up of our thoughts, beliefs, and self-talk—are always "on." According to scientists, we have about 60,000 thoughts a day. That's *one thought per second during every waking hour.* No wonder we're so tired at the end of the day!

And what's even more startling is that of those 60,000 thoughts, 95 percent are the same thoughts you had yesterday, and the day before, and the day before that. Your mind is like a record player playing the same record over and over again.

Talk about being stuck in a rut!

Still, that wouldn't be so bad if it weren't for the next statistic: For the average person, 80 percent of those habitual thoughts are *negative.* That means that every day most people have more than 45,000 negative thoughts … Dr. Daniel Amen, a world-renowned psychiatrist and brain imaging specialist, calls them automatic negative thoughts, or ANTs.

So what is the impact of 45,000 ANTS bombarding our minds every day?

It's not good!

Quantum physics has shown that we actually create our own reality.

Stay with me.

This means that what we entertain in our minds creates seeds that later bear fruit, which then becomes a part of our existence. The long and short of it is that, through our thought lives, we impact our situations—for good or for bad!

In other words, we become what we think!

Does that mean we are at the mercy of what is in our minds, thus our resulting negative reality is predetermined?

No!

Epigenetics studies effects not encoded in the DNA sequence of an organism. Experts in that field have found that, not only do our genes control the color of our eyes, but also our behavior and personality traits. They've found that, contrary to what we used to believe, we can impact our genes.

Now isn't the time to discuss all that is involved in this process, but the oversimplified bottom line is that experts in the field of epigenetics have proven that when we interpret life events in a positive way, we will think positive things. And in doing so, we will actually change the chemical makeup of our minds and even reform our genes. And this, in turn, impacts our behaviors.

We become what we think! Because what we think is what we believe—it is our reality!

Every thought releases brain chemicals. Being focused on negative thoughts effectively saps the brain of its positive forcefulness, slows it down, and can go as far as dimming its ability to function, even creating depression.

On the flip side, thinking positive, happy, hopeful, optimistic, joyful thoughts decreases cortisol and produces serotonin, which creates a sense of well-being. This helps the brain function at peak capacity.

Happy thoughts and positive thinking, in general, support brain growth, as well as the generation and reinforcement of new synapses, especially in the prefrontal cortex (PFC), which serves as the integration center of all brain-mind function.

Whew!

Now let's take that science lesson and apply it to you and me.

Who decides what is stored in our minds?

We do!

And when we store "good" things, good things happen.

Schimoff goes on to say the following:

Have the intention to notice everything good that happens to you: any positive thought you have, anything you see, feel, taste, hear, or smell that brings you pleasure, a win you experience, a breakthrough in your understanding about something, an expression of your creativity—the list goes on and on. This intention activates the reticular activating system (RAS), a group of cells at the base of your brain stem responsible for sorting through the massive amounts of incoming information and bringing anything important to your attention. Have you ever bought a car and then suddenly started noticing the same make of car everywhere? It's the RAS at work. Now you can use it to be happier. When you decide to look for the positive, your RAS makes sure that's what you see.

So, how do we do that?

Here is one thing that I do. Every night, as I am closing my day, I write in my journal one positive experience that I had that day. When I do that, I am activating my reticular activation system and flooding it with positivity.

When we flood our reticular activation systems with positive information, we are happy.

When we are happy, good things happen.

Which makes us happy.

And then more good things happen!

Now, that is a cycle that anyone can appreciate!

A few months after my first doctor's visit, I found myself sitting in his office in that same chair, relaxed, smiling, and ready to interact. I had been going in regularly for consultation and monitoring. After about forty-five minutes of probing questions, my doctor looked up and said, "I don't see any evidence that you are suffering from the symptoms of Bipolar II in your behavior, words, or thought life. I am completely amazed at the progress you have made. Your commitment to getting healthy has been something I rarely see. Congratulations!"

I am not so haughty as to think that I will not struggle with bipolar issues again. Mental health is such a squishy thing, and there is so much about it that we don't understand.

I am so thankful that there are those who have dedicated themselves to finding out the causes of and finding the solutions for mental illness.

I have begun to learn how to register events in my life—how to interpret them and how to handle them. I am learning how to take every thought captive and make sure that my thoughts aren't sinking me.

Do you know what that means?

When I catch myself entertaining a negative thought, I imagine myself catching it inside an air bubble. Instead of letting that thought run rampant and unchecked through my mind, I immediately identify it as negative, and I don't allow myself to consider it further. I actually visualize myself encircling it in a bubble, and I letting it float away.

For me, it is making all the difference in the world.

I invite you to give it a go.

A great way to practice is to find a time and place where you can quietly sit. Just listen to your breath. See if you can count ten breaths without letting your thoughts distract you.

When a thought comes, don't berate yourself. Simply envelop it in a little cloud or bubble and let it float away. Then return to counting your breath.

Every morning, I do a variation of this for at least ten minutes. Sometimes I sit and consider a positive word or truth. Try it. It may just be the first step in cleaning up your mind.

Also, at the end of each day I write down one positive experience that I have had in the last twenty-four hours. This helps my mind focus on what is good instead of whatever negative thing may have happened to me during the day.

Death and life are in the power of the tongue.

Jewish Proverb

Sticks and stones may break my bones, but words can kill or heal me!

Doug Clark

CHAPTER 5

Ouch:
The Power of Words!

It was my distinct honor to serve in the Arizona Legislature as a state representative. Being an elected official was not easy; 50 percent of the people were always mad at you. This week, a particular group may like you. But last week, because you voted contrary to their opinion, they were calling for your head.

I remember a particularly difficult period where, as legislators, we were wrestling with some very difficult issues. The meetings were long, the debate intense. We were trying our best to come up with a resolution that would pass. We had all received scathing e-mails and voicemails from constituents claiming their side of the issue as the only true solution.

The words were ugly. Some of the repeatable ones went like this: "You guys are incompetent;" "You should be ashamed of yourself;" and "How did you ever get elected?"

We were starting to believe those messages.

After a particularly long session, I was in the restroom, splashing water on my face and trying to get refreshed. Others were doing the same. All of a sudden, one of my colleagues, standing in front of the mirror, looked at his reflection and declared, "I'm good enough, I'm smart enough, and doggone it, people like me!"

We roared!

Tears rolled down our faces as we found release in the moment.

Why is that?

It's because words have an impact.

A while back, I was visiting my parents at their home in Yakima, Washington, and my dad was walking me around the property they had recently acquired. It was the first real estate they had ever purchased. I was so proud of them.

They were able to obtain it for a great price because of the work that needed to be done on it. The house and the lot were a complete dump. But they cleaned it up and remodeled the inside and outside of the structure.

On this particular day, my dad was showing me what they had been working on outside and what they had accomplished. As we rounded the corner of the garage, he pointed out an area of ground that had been recently tilled. A garden!

Fantastic.

The Yakima Valley was known for its produce. It had fertile ground, plentiful water, and a great summertime growing temperature.

However, his garden was in an odd spot, back behind the garage, in an area that would not get optimum sunshine. It almost seemed hidden.

"I put it here in case I failed," my dad told me.

Ouch!

Why would anyone worry about failing at gardening? People fail at it all the time. Even people who have had gardens for years have experienced seasons where nothing comes up!

I think I know why. You see, as my father grew up, his dad always told him he was inadequate, a failure.

His father always spoke in demeaning ways to him. His father would continually call him stupid and incapable and repeatedly told him he'd fail in all his efforts.

After years and years of that kind of treatment, my father began to believe it. So much so that, even as an adult, he was tentatively starting a garden. But, only where no one could see it—lest he fail.

You remember the childhood chant, "Sticks and stones may break my bones, but words will never hurt me!"

I want to go on record and say that's bologna!

Words hurt like mad. I don't care how old you are. Ugly, negative, hurtful words do damage.

We have all experienced the sting of hurtful words.

Whether it was on the playground at school, with our neighbor, our employer, our significant other.

You stink!

You are incompetent!

You will never amount to anything!

You're a loser!

Thrown at us like a spear to our hearts, not only do those words hurt at the time, but they also sometimes stick around with incredible precision and sound quality; those same negative, hurtful words play like a tape recorder in our minds.

When I was young my grandmother used to teasingly ask all of us grandkids, "What are you good for? You're good for nothing aren't you?"

She meant no harm. She loved and valued us. However, decades later, those words came roaring back to me and brought me to tears during a counseling session. I'd finally recognized that I had been trying for years to prove to her and everyone else that I *was* good for something!

How powerful are words?

Through the 1990s, Dr. Masaru Emoto performed a series of experiments observing the physical effect of words. He used the crystalline structure of water as his object.

Emoto hired photographers to take high-resolution pictures of water after being exposed to different words. The results were nothing short of remarkable.

This is what Emoto said about his discovery:

We refer to the crystalline structure of water as "clusters." The smaller the clusters, the healthier the water. [We found that] slang words like "you fool" destroy clusters. You would not see any crystals in these cases. Negative phrases and words create large clusters or will not form clusters, and positive, beautiful words and phrases create small, tight clusters.

From these experiments, we have come to the conclusion that the water is reacting to the actual words. For example, for our trip to Europe we used the words "thank you" and "you fool" in German. The people on our team who took the actual photographs of the water crystals did not understand the German for "you fool," and yet the same results occurred based on the words used.

After observing these miraculous results, Dr. Emoto went on to *write* out different words, both positive and negative in nature:

"You make me sick."

"I will kill you."

"Thank you."

"Love and appreciation."

He then *taped* the words to containers full of water.

The results were incredible!

Emoto continues,

The water stamped with positive, beautiful words and phrases had smaller, tighter crystalline clusters (healthier) and was far more symmetrical and aesthetically pleasing than that stamped with dark, negative phrases and words, which had either large clusters (unhealthy) or no crystalline clusters at all.

"Healthy" water broke apart when negative words were spoken to it. While "unhealthy," polluted water improved in quality when positive words were spoken to it.

Oh, and by the way, the average human body is about 60 percent water. Ponder that one for a while.

What Emoto's study showed was that positive and negative words have an impact on us—and on the surrounding environment.

Although we may not be able to see its impact with the naked eye, his astounding and tangible evidence can help us understand the impact of words.

If the words that come out of us have this effect on water crystals, it's amazing to think about the kind of effect they could have on the people and events that come into our lives.

By speaking positive words, words of affirmation and truth, we can actually improve our well-being (and the well-being of others) and, as a result, have a healthier, more meaningful, enjoyable life.

And so the old folk saying should be, "Sticks and stones may break my bones but words can heal or kill me!"

As I grew up, my parents continually lifted me up the best they could and empowered me with their words. They constantly told me that there wasn't anything I could not do.

There was a period in my life, however, when they were not happy with the value system I was forming. During that time they would say, "We are not happy with how you turned out!"

I still remember the sting of those words.

Did they really mean that? No, of course not. But, in that instant of time, that is what they were feeling and they spoke it aloud.

And unfortunately, those words, along with the playful teasing of my grandmother, and all the other negative statements people said to me over the years, began to add up.

Those words became a powerful negative soundtrack that I started believing.

Interestingly, while we can be impacted externally both negatively and positively by words that are spoken to us - the largest impact comes from the words that we speak to ourselves.

I found that my internal dialogue had been poisoned.

How?

I had let circumstances and events take on a negative hue.

I began saying things to myself like, *Well, Doug, what more is there? The chances of you accomplishing anything more are pretty slim.*

As I mentioned earlier in this book, I'd reached a point in my life where I began telling people, "I'm okay to die now."

I would tell them I'd experienced more in my fifty years than the normal person. That I'd accomplished more than most. And that it would be selfish of me to expect more out of life.

What would drive me to make those kinds of statements?

What I was really feeling inside was a lot of doubt. I really didn't know if I could do anything more. I didn't know if I could measure up. I didn't know if I was good enough to accomplish anything else.

Negative words had swamped my mental boat and were sinking me.

It was a constant struggle for my father to block out the negative words of his youth. My grandfather had polluted and destroyed the "water" in my dad's mind by endlessly telling him that he was a failure. My dad believed those words and thus was afraid to put his garden where anyone could see it. He believed he probably would fail.

And failing would confirm what his dad had always said about him.

I am so proud of my dad in that arena.

In spite of the continual berating and belittling that he endured as a child, he succeeded in so much more than just planting a garden.

In fact, just recently I received a Facebook message from, Oscar, a young man whom my father had impacted at a young age. This young man came from a very difficult background. He lived in the poorest of slums called 'La Chacarita' in Asuncion, the capital city of Paraguay. He didn't know who his dad was, and like many his age in that area, he belonged to a gang.

This is how I met Oscar: my father rushed into my room in the middle of the night and shook me awake. He told me that he needed to go to The Chacarita—right now—and needed me to go with him.

The Chacarita was a drug-infested, impoverished area of town known for its gang activity, where literally thousands of people lived in cardboard boxes.

Oscar had been beaten up and had sent word to my father. My father knew it was unwise to go to that area alone, and that's why he needed me to accompany him.

On the drive, we talked about Oscar. My father had taken him under his wing—no doubt identifying with his challenging situation—and had become a dad to him. And when Oscar was in trouble, he would reach out to the man who had shown him love, the man who knew he could become so much more than what his surroundings dictated.

When we reconnected via social media, the first thing Oscar did was asked was if I could please send his love to his "dad." Oscar is now helping others, who, like himself, come from a tough background. He works through a prison outreach, connecting with inmates at a jail in Ciudad Del Este, Paraguay.

So, what words were spoken into your life? Are they negative words that beat you down?

Don't listen to them!

What words do you speak to yourself? Are you speaking negative words? Do you continually berate yourself?

Stop!

Don't listen to that negative voicemail. It is, in essence, poisoning you!

Replace the negative words with positive ones.

Here is my new practice. I speak words of affirmation to myself. And, when possible, I don't just think those words of affirmation about myself. Sometimes, like when

I am driving, I state them aloud. I sing them or even shout them out, as if I am at a ball game.

I use each letter of the alphabet as a guide for my affirming statements. For example:

A: I am awesome!

B: I am bold!

C: I am capable!

D: I am diligent!

E: I am excellent!

F: I am fantastic!

You get the idea.

Sometimes I get creative and try to think of multiple affirmations for each letter; when I can't think of another affirmation, I just simply go to the next letter in the alphabet.

It is amazing what these words do to my mental, emotional, and yes, even my physical, well-being.

Notice, I don't beat myself up and say, "You stupid idiot, you should be able to think of more positive words that begin with 'B.' What a loser you are."

That would defeat the whole practice, wouldn't it?

The other practice I do is look for opportunities to speak affirming words to others.

My father passed away recently.

As I sat in his memorial service, it struck me as odd that we were saying all kinds of nice things about a person who was no longer with us.

It was nice, and helpful, to be reminded of my father's positive attributes. But I can tell you, without a shadow of a doubt, he would have loved to hear those affirmations with his own ears.

So, that is what I try to do.

As I go through my day, I try to speak affirming words to as many people as I can.

Sometimes I write an affirming note to someone on a note card and mail it to him or her.

Yep, an actual letter with stamps and everything!

I don't write anything big or fantastic. But because words are powerful, I know that whatever I speak or write can bring encouragement and health.

To keep this in my mind, each day when I write in my journal, I record an affirmation that I spoke or wrote in the last twenty-four hours.

The next time you catch yourself saying "You idiot;" "You knucklehead;" or "You fool" to yourself, realize that those words have impact!

Change them; say phrases to yourself like "I'm still learning;" "I'm still trying;" and "I can do this."

It won't take long before you start noticing a change in your perspective. Instead of feeling that you will probably fail, you will start finding success in your attempts and also begin to see positive results!

I know you can do it, I believe in you!

"It is not good for man to live alone."

God

CHAPTER 6

Lone Ranger:
The Power of Connection

Remember the Lone Ranger, the celebrated icon of our youth? This masked hero who came from nowhere on his white horse and saved the day was celebrated not just because of his heroic actions, but because of he was seemingly able to do everything largely by himself. Even his name highlighted the fact that he apparently didn't need anyone else. The "Lone Ranger!"

Have you ever considered how, at a gas station in the middle of the wilderness, on a two-lane gas station suddenly two, three or even four travelers will stop to get gas at the same time?

My grandfather used to run a gas station. I remember talking to him about his work. One thing that stuck out as strange in his mind was how the station would be completely empty of cars needing gas and then all at once a group of cars would come in. This was back in the days before traffic lights which group us together in clusters and could possibly explain why we arrive at a gas station in waves today.

We never did talk about why he thought that was, but it was intriguing to me that would be something that made an impression on him about his work.

Since that time, I have spent time watching this phenomenon as I have crisscrossed the country by car. It amazes me to watch it occur. I invite you the next time you schedule your 'get away' to carve out some time and observe this occurrence.

Here is another one. Why is it that preteens and teenagers always walk around in clumps. Visit any fast-food restaurant during the lunch break of a nearby high school and you will witness this phenomenon.

While on the one hand this example of connectivity could seem to be mere coincidence, we have all experienced the joy of connection and the loneliness of disconnection.

During my Perfect Storm I was overwhelmed with a sense of disconnectedness.

I was out of sync.

I didn't fit in.

I remember trying to explain this to someone and I said, "I'm looking for my tribe."

I began to wonder, why does it even bother me that I am 'disconnected'. What was causing me to feel disconnected? And conversely, what does it mean to be 'connected'? Is it necessary? Why did I long to be 'Connected'? When would I know that I am 'connected'?

Because I didn't feel connected, I felt awkward in social settings. I started wanting to be alone. While it is understood that a measured regular time alone can actually be healthy, that definitely isn't what was going on with me.

The crazy thing was that while on the one hand I felt like I wanted to be secluded and alone, on the other hand I felt extremely lonely and disconnected. It was a weird paradox. I didn't want to be with anyone... and yet at the same time, I did!

In the novel 'The Martian', Watney is left stranded and utterly alone on Mars because of a number of unfortunate oversights and circumstances. While the work of surviving initially keeps him occupied, his days and nights soon become repetitive, boring and empty. Though Watney rarely says so, many of his actions reveal his desire for human connection.

Anthony Robbins believes that central to our experience of fulfillment in life is to authentically love and make deep connections with other living beings. Does that resonate with you?

The story is told of when Winkie Pratney was being visited by a friend. At the time Winkie, a researcher who has a background in organic research chemistry, was conducting an experiment trying to find if plants have feelings.

All of a sudden, the monitors on his plants started going off the charts with indications of distress and alarm. Winkie had no idea why. He looked across to his friend and saw that his friend was picking at a scab on the back of his hand.

Einstein discovered that two particles that used to be next to each other in the past and then subsequently were separated to a large distance – still appear to maintain a strange kind of connection. Einstein called it "spooky action at a distance."

Now quantum physics has begun to show that there is a "kind of quantum linkage between all particles, even those who haven't interacted in the past. In fact, they have no idea that the other particle even existed." Says Jeff Tollaksen, Director for the Institute for Quantum Studies at Chapman University.

What does all this mean to you and me?

It shows that even at our most basic human existence, the smallest particle of who we are, is cosmically connected to the other particles of the universe. And when that connection is broken, or strained, or starved, those particles react and yearn for reconnection.

All living creatures and plants are connected somehow. And even when we are 'disconnected' we are still 'connected'. When a 'disconnect' in us or someone else happens we 'feel' it. We are not meant to live in isolation. We benefit from being connected to others. To have relationship with other humans at the very least and even with animals and plants.

While we live in a time of human existence when we are supposedly more connected than ever due to social media. We really have lost the true meaning of connection. Unfortunately, we have lost that in our culture today. Most everything we do is geared to keeping us as isolated individuals.

Can I correct our thinking about the Lone Ranger? Did you know how he got his name? We always think it is because he preferred to be alone – thus the name 'Lone' Ranger. But here is the real story. The Lone Ranger got his name because he was the 'lone' surviving Ranger of a brutal attack. And his companion 'Tonto' wasn't just an afterthought who assisted the Lone Ranger in his adventures. Tonto actually nursed the Lone Ranger back to life and in that way the two bonded.

When the Lone Ranger was back on his feet, they committed to go through life together doing good.

There is a reason you are tired of being a 'Lone Ranger' – you weren't meant to be alone. You are a Survivor. You have survived your perfect storm for a purpose.

Have you ever felt disconnected? I am certain you have. There is a very high probability that as you navigate you perfect storm you are feeling disconnected right now.

It is normal to long for connection. Don't stuff it down. Acknowledge it. And take steps to resolve it. Join a club. Invite someone out for coffee. Make yourself vulnerable to another human. Show another human that you care about them. All of these acts foster connection, which in turn will foster a sense of well being in you.

Be open to finding your Tonto, your Tribe, and commit to go through life together doing good.

My best friend is the friend who brings out the best in me.

Henry Ford

CHAPTER 7

One Bad Apple:
The Power of Friends!

Eating healthfully is a high priority for me. So, most weekday mornings, I make myself a smoothie for breakfast out of fresh fruits and vegetables. Now, weekends are a different story! Fried eggs, bacon, and hash browns are my go-to breakfast comfort food.

But I digress!

I set up my NutriBullet to make my morning smoothie and begin to pick the ingredients.

First, I choose a green: kale, mixed greens, collard greens, spinach, or romaine.

Then, I add a few different types of fruit: bananas, strawberries, pineapples, apples, or peaches.

Then I put in some nuts, flaxseed, and goji berries, add water, and then twist the canister into the base so that it blends.

It seems that every day, I have to sort through the berries because invariably one or more of them has begun to rot and mold has begun to grow.

I pick out the bad ones and throw them away. If I'm not attentive and don't do this regularly, when I grab a handful of berries, I will find that a whole group of berries has gone bad. Invariably, there is one berry in the middle that seems to be more rotten than the rest.

What is going on?

We've all heard the saying that one bad apple spoils the whole barrel, but does that actually happen? Can one bad apple really ruin the whole barrel?

Actually, yes.

As they ripen, some fruits, like apples and pears, produce a gaseous hormone called ethylene, which is, among other things, a ripening agent.

When you store fruits together, the ethylene emitted from each separate piece prods the others around them to ripen further, and vice versa.

Fun tip: Want to quickly ripen an avocado? Stick it in a paper bag with an apple overnight.

The riper a piece of fruit is, the more ethylene it produces, eventually leading to a gas concentration level powerful enough to over-ripen all nearby fruit.

Given the right conditions and enough time, one apple *can* push all the fruit around it to ripen—and eventually rot.

Additionally, a mold-infested piece of fruit will contaminate nearby fruit, as the mold seeks additional food sources and spreads.

In both cases, it actually does take just one single bad apple to start a domino chain that ruins the rest of the bunch.

The same thing happens to us as humans. No, we won't go bad if we hang out with an overripe apple; however, just like one apple can affect another apple, the humans with whom we associate impact us.

For example, back in my high school days, my sister used to constantly tell me, "Quit being just like Vic!"

Vic was my buddy. He was everyone's buddy. He was always good for a laugh. And as a freshman in high school, I highly valued that characteristic. I wanted everyone to like me, and Vic seemed to have the magic recipe to make that happen.

Easygoing and lackadaisical, he was kind of roly-poly with a chipmunk smile. He didn't really walk. He kind of just glided to his destination.

He could shrug his shoulders in just the right way. The perfect quips, brush-offs, and one-liners were continually flowing from his lips. And I became his perfect student!

I became easygoing and lackadaisical. I learned to glide down the walkway, smile like a chipmunk, shrug my shoulders, and quickly dispense quips, brush-offs, and one-liners.

Vic had some other characteristics that I also picked up. He had a hard time making it to the classroom before the tardy bell. But, hey it wasn't easy to glide, shrug your shoulders, and make everyone laugh—and still make it to class on time.

He didn't take school seriously. Didn't do his homework. Didn't study for tests. And why should he—he didn't take anything seriously.

Unfortunately, I also began to pick up those characteristics. Class? In a bit. Homework? Maybe tomorrow! Test? You've got to be kidding!

My As soon became Bs, and my grades were headed in a downward direction.

And although my sister was alluding to my attempts to mirror his mannerisms and humor, it would have been appropriate for her to tell me to quit being like Vic in any way!

What happened? Bad company ruins good character. I'm not saying that Vic was a bad person. But he definitely had some values, habits, and outlooks that were not optimal if one wanted to graduate from high school.

I realized that although, in my short-sightedness, I wanted to be liked, I really didn't want to do my freshman year over again.

I saw the light. I decided to hang out with Sam and David. Solid guys. Good students. Self-disciplined. Well-behaved. A good measure of humor mixed with level-headedness.

The end result was that I graduated—in the normally allotted time period!

What happened? Fortunately, the reverse is also true: good company encourages good character. Just as bad company can ruin good character, good company can encourage good character! This is what Epictetus believed. You remember him don't you?

Epictetus was a Greek-speaking Stoic philosopher. He was born a slave and lived in Rome until his banishment, and then he went to northwestern Greece where he lived for the rest of his life.

Epictetus is known for saying, "The key is to keep company only with people who uplift you, whose presence calls forth your best."

He argued that all external events are uncontrollable but that we are responsible for our own actions and attitudes, which we examine and control through self-discipline.

He also believed that who we choose to hang out with impacts our attitudes, which in turn impact our actions and eventually becomes the measure of our character.

Working backward:

- Our character is proven by our actions.

- Our actions are determined by our attitude.
- Our attitude is impacted by those with whom we associate.

Following this logic, it is important for us to learn how to examine our personal relationships and determine which ones are good for us. Ask yourself the following questions:

- How do you feel after spending time with your friend?
- What attitudes do you have?
- How do you find yourself approaching life?

Have you ever felt energized after having visited with someone? How about the reverse? Have you ever left, totally drained, after having visited with someone?

Are there people in your life that you just can't wait to spend time with? Are there people in your life that you dread spending time with and you have to mentally prepare yourself before answering their calls or visiting their homes?

Gordon MacDonald, in his book *Ordering Your Private World*, describes different kinds of people that exist in our lives. I've listed them below and added to his original thoughts:

Very Resourceful People (VRPs): These are the people who ignite your passion. These are mentors, coaches, and trusted advocates who help you grow in your skill and wisdom. They invigorate you and cause you to want to be better.

- *Very Important People (VIPs)*: They share your passion. These are teammates, close friends. VIPs encourage you, sharpen you, hold you accountable, and collaborate with you to achieve your goals.

- *Very Trainable People (VTPs)*: These people catch your passion. They want to grow. These are the people whom you can invest in because they are teachable.

- *Very Nice People (VNPs)*: They are just that. They enjoy your passion but add little to your life. They don't share your passion. They are wonderful to be with and are often encouraging. But they don't challenge you, and they don't contribute to your life. They are good for your ego but generally just want to receive.

- *Very Draining People (VDPs)*: These drain your passion. They are "emotional black holes" who will easily consume most of your time and energy if you let them. They are needy people who drain you of your strength and time. They tend to be negative complainers.

As you read Gordon's designations, did a name or a face come to mind?

It has been a privilege to have some very resourceful and important people in my life. I have found that when I spend time with them, my outlook improves. My energy is optimized. My curiosity is piqued. I get more out of my day. I get more out of life!

It has also been a joy to have very trainable people in my life; ones into whom I can pour whatever I know.

What a joy to also have a myriad of very nice people who have encouraged me to keep going.

And yes, there have been very draining people in my life; people who seemed to just drain the life right out of me.

I am currently working through these designations and purposefully identifying the people in my life that fit into each category.

I want to maximize the impact that the VRPs and the VIPs have on my life. I want to be measured in the exposure I have with VDPs.

So, I invite you to take inventory of your own relationships:

- Who are the resourceful people who ignite your passion?
- Who are the inspiring people?
- Who are your trainable people?
- Who are the nice people?
- And last of all, who in your life drains the energy out of you?

As you identify them, think about the time you spend with each friendship that you have and assess it:

- You really want to maximize your VRP and VIP relationships.
- You want to invest wisely in the VTP relationships.

- Make sure you appreciate but balance the VNP relationships.

- Certainly, minimize the time spent in the VDP relationships.

Conversely, make steps to be a giver in your relationships so that you don't become a VDP. My goal is to never be less than a "Very Trainable Person" to anyone in my life.

Make steps to be nice but don't inflate someone's ego—be loyal and honest. Be trainable; listen, learn, grow.

Be inspiring to others; come alongside and share passion with others.

Be a resource; be generous with your wisdom, knowledge, and energy.

Let's minimize our exposure to the bad apples in our lives and make sure we are good apples in the lives of others!

And guess what?

There is another benefit to having healthy friendships: life longevity.

While exercise and quitting smoking are thought to be important steps for a long, healthy life, a new study by researcher Julianne Hold- Lunstad, a psychologist at Brigham Young University suggests another potential tip for extending our lifespan: make some friends.

Results from this study show that people with strong social relationships increased their odds of survival over a certain time period by 50 percent. That is on par with ceasing to smoke and nearly twice as beneficial as physical activity in terms of decreasing your odds of dying early.

The question I'd like you to ask yourself is whether there is someone in your life whom you would feel comfortable phoning at four in the morning to tell your troubles to.

If your answer is yes, you will likely live longer than someone whose answer is no.

Let's live longer—let's make friends!

To err is human; to forgive, divine.

Alexander Pope

CHAPTER 8

Drinking Poison:

The Power of Forgiveness!

I sat and watched her make her way to her door with strong feelings of respect and honor, mixed with disappointment and regret.

We had just shared a weekend in California. Nothing romantic - just friends. "Right!" you say.

No, seriously.

And not only that—the woman I am speaking of is my ex-wife!

She and I had spent the Fourth of July weekend with my, or more correctly—our—youngest son and his soon-to be-bride.

Yes, you read correctly. I had just gone on a twelve hour road trip and spent the weekend with my ex-wife. No anger, no hatred, no vitriol, no digs.

What's up with that?

Forgiveness.

As I briefly mentioned in chapter 1, my marriage of twenty-five years had fallen apart. I refused then—and I refuse now—to get into the details of what went wrong, who was to blame, pointing fingers, the "he said, she said."

I will, however, take full responsibility for everything I did or did not do that caused our marriage to fall apart.

It was only a few months before this weekend trip, while we were on a hike together, when I verbalized what was rolling around inside my mind.

I expressed to her how appreciative I was of her effort to make our marriage work. I told her that she had done an incredible job of mothering our boys.

And, I told her that, in spite of our inability to keep our marriage intact, I truly valued the friendship that we had created out of the ashes of that failure. With no intention of manipulating our friendship into something else, I asked if she would forgive me for my failures as a husband and a father.

She very graciously forgave me and asked for my forgiveness for her failures as a wife and a mother. I forgave her and we agreed that we would do everything we could to build a friendship out of what had been a beautiful marriage.

That act created the opportunity, even the desire, to spend that weekend together, with our son and his girlfriend in celebration of their engagement.

Forgiveness is powerful.

I am certain you have heard the saying that withholding forgiveness is like drinking poison and hoping the other person gets sick.

That is so true.

Why?

What is so important about forgiveness?

Research has shown that not forgiving can lead to

- spiritual and psychological hindrances;
- anxiety, stress, and hostility;
- higher blood pressure;
- depression;
- autoimmune deficiencies;
- heart issues;
- lower self-esteem; and
- unhealthy relationships.

Do you have any of those in your life? Do you want to get rid of them?

Learning to forgive may just help you!

None of us have reached this point in life without having had someone offend, hurt, or worse yet abuse us.

A client of mine had been abused by her father when she was young. While that abuse in and of itself is tragic enough – and should never happen – when she told her mother what had had happened her mother simply stated, 'We will never talk about this again!'

For years she lived with the sting of two offenses, the original abuse and the unwillingness of a parent to deal with it correctly. If there ever was a valid reason to not forgive, this would be at the top of the list.

Later in life her father begged her to forgive him. At first she refused to do so. However, as we talked she was able to see that she was only harming herself. She forgave him and before his recent death was able to have some treasured, healthy, moments with him.

Her mother, unfortunately, never admitted that she handled the situation incorrectly. My client had the opportunity to hold on to the offense, or forgive, even though her mother was not asking for forgiveness.

I am so happy to say that she chose to forgive. Unfortunately, the relationship between mother and daughter was never restored – but that was because of another reason that we will discuss later.

Who do you need to forgive?

As you go through your day and a picture of someone comes to mind, notice your feelings about him or her.

Do you remember all the good times you have had with them? The fun? The value they bring to you?

Or do you immediately remember what they did wrong to you?

A person that I am learning to forgive is a person who is partially responsible for my financial collapse. This friend – well to be honest I don't really consider him a friend any more- is a Real estate mogul in my home state. He was in a sticky spot with a large piece of property that he ends on the north end of town. He had been leasing it from the state and the lease was about to end. However, he didn't want to lose the income that was coming from the property.

He asked if I would serve as his Real Estate agent negotiate a sale with the State. He said, "Doug, I promise you a huge commission! You will be looking at well over $200,000.' I agreed to this role. And because he was my friend, the agreement was sealed with a handshake and I went to work.

I invested hundreds of hours into the transaction. Working through mind numbing pages of documents to make sure my client's interests were protected.

What a surprise it was to me when the transaction successfully closed a year later to receive a letter from his lawyer saying they would not be paying me any commission but here was a check for $1000.00 as a thank you for my efforts. My friend denied ever making that commitment to me and I continually kick myself for not having put the agreement in writing.

I sometimes think how different things might have been if I had received that money. We all know that money cannot buy happiness, but it can take care of a lot of life's stresses!

I do my best to forgive him each time I think of what happened. It is an exercise for me.

Without too much effort I can picture three other people in my mind who I feel did me wrong.

These are people who I have had incredible life experiences with. Friends I have laughed with, cried with, shared the joys and pains of life with.

Yet I know I need to forgive them because the first picture or feeling have toward them is negative because of the hurt I feel they caused.

Man, it isn't easy.

But I am continuing to work on it. I have asked all three if they would sit down with me and work through what has come between us.

One declined, and one has yet to respond. That has given me another opportunity to learn to forgive.

Now, I have their response—or lack thereof—along with the original "infraction."

The third person asked for forgiveness via e-mail and I forgave—kind of.

Really, I have only partially forgiven all of them.

What do I mean by that?

Well, one day I think I've forgiven them, and the next day, when their faces come across my mind, I find I am still angry at what they did.

It's like I am holding a grudge against them.

Holding a grudge is merely an expression of lack of forgiveness.

It doesn't impact the person that you are holding the grudge against, but if not dealt with, it certainly fills you with poison—and leads to bitterness. The only person that I am hurting by not forgiving is myself.

So, forgive, I must!

And really, why not forgive? The act of forgiveness brings so many benefits. As I forgive, I find that I will have

- healthier relationships;
- greater spiritual and psychological well-being;
- less anxiety, stress, and hostility;
- lower blood pressure;
- fewer symptoms of depression;
- a stronger immune system;
- improved heart health; and
- higher self-esteem.

Without even knowing you, I know there is a person who has let you down and who needs forgiveness: yourself.

Remember the story earlier in this chapter about my client who forgave her mother for mishandling the fact that husband was abusing their daughter? Remember I said that although the daughter eventually forgave the mom, the relationship was never restored?

Here is why: the mom never forgave herself!

While the act of forgiving others is crucial, the act of forgiving ourselves is equally important. And in fact, in my opinion, forgiving ourselves really needs to happen first.

Why?

Because if we can't forgive ourselves, it is next to impossible to truly forgive others.

So, do you forgive yourself?

I have a love/hate relationship with personality assessments and behavior profiles that are popular and, I might add, helpful.

There are a number of them out there, and I think I have taken most of them! Some of the more popular ones are Myers-Briggs, DISC, StrengthsFinder, and Predictive Index.

But the summary that I get from all of them is that I pay enough attention to details so I can minimize mistakes and strive to be the best; so that I can win. I love to win, and I love to be first. I tend to view everything as a competition. And as I look back on my life, that has been true.

I have paid meticulous attention to details and pushed myself so that I could be my best. And also so I can be recognized as one of the best at whatever it is I am doing.

However, I have some first-place prizes in my life that I am not proud of in the least.

I feel my failed marriage is one of those.

No one else in my immediate family has experienced divorce. My very own parents exemplified commitment and tenacity, jointly working through difficult issues. They went on to celebrate fifty-seven years of marriage.

Many other of my close relatives were able to slog through difficulties and remain married. I am only aware of a cousin of a cousin of a cousin of a cousin (you get the idea) who got a divorce.

The personality assessments also state that if I am not successful, I have a strong tendency to beat myself up, bathing in guilt.

For many years, I did just that almost on a daily basis over my failed marriage. I continually imagined the things that I could have done differently, things that might have helped it successfully last a lifetime. I declared myself guilty in the court of my mind.

Let me further illustrate.

As a dad, I wanted to be the best. I wanted to win "Father of the Year" every year. When either of my boys got in trouble, I would immediately pin the blame on myself. It was my fault! I was the guilty one.

For the longest time, even after both of my sons had grown and moved out on there own, when either one of them made a decision that didn't mesh with my value system, or they made a choice that I believed was be less than best—I drew an arrow straight to myself. I concluded that something I said or modeled probably caused them to make that decision.

I took a magnifying glass to actions that I had taken, examined the words that I had spoken to them, as they were growing up. I continually identified what *I did* and then hammered myself with what I felt *I should have done.*

I even tried to create mistakes. Maybe I did that wrong. Maybe they misunderstood when I said or did that.

And then I filled myself up with guilt.

Do you do the same thing?

Guilt is obsessing about something that happened in the past! We can't change history, so we need to quit feeling guilty about it!

How?

Forgive ourselves!

That's what I had to learn how to do.

Until we are able to forgive ourselves, I question whether we can truly, and fully, forgive others.

Forgiveness is really for my benefit, not necessarily for the benefit of others. Forgiveness offers me peace. Forgiveness gives me the opportunity to stop judging, to stop condemning.

Forgiveness is a gift I give myself.

The person who will benefit is you! So, join me, let's forgive those that have offended us.

Cultivate the habit of being grateful for every good thing that comes to you, and to give thanks continuously. And because all things have contributed to your advancement, you should include all things in your gratitude.

Ralph Waldo Emerson

In all things give thanks, for this is the will of God concerning you!

Apostle Paul

CHAPTER 9

Saying Thank You:
The Power of Gratitude!

"Hmmmm, what do I have to be thankful for?" I asked myself.

Each evening, I set time aside to write down three things that I am thankful for.

I'm sitting with a tablet of paper on my lap, pen in my hand, and I am having a hard time coming up with things to be thankful for.

Instead, I am feeling claustrophobic. Lost. Alone. Stranded. Disenfranchised. Listless. Uncared for. Disconnected. Lacking.

Seriously?

I am having a hard time finding things to be thankful for?

Try this on: I am sitting with a tablet of paper on my lap and a pen in my hand. That means I am probably able to read and write. It also means that I have a chair to sit on. It means I'm alive! Isn't that enough?

Allow me to paint the whole picture for you.

I am sitting—get this—on the seventh-floor balcony of the apartment where I am staying for the next four months. There is a fresh summer breeze blowing across my face; the moon is kissing my cheek. Birds are chirping delightfully just feet from me.

There is a spectacular view to the east where, every morning, I get to see the sun rise over the mountains. In fact, the whole east wall of my residence is floor-to-ceiling glass. And luscious green plants frame the entire picture.

I awoke this morning after a great night's sleep, where I didn't have to worry about my safety (unlike at my last place). Nor was I woken up by the resident above me using the restroom at 2:00 a.m. (also unlike my last place).

I enjoyed a great smoothie made from fresh fruit and vegetables. I had taken a warm shower and made myself a delicious cup of coffee.

That is just what happened the first part of my day. And yet—I am having a hard time finding something to be grateful for.

How can that be?

It's because I had begun to expect these things.

Unfortunately, that is human nature. When we receive something on a regular basis, we typically begin to take it for granted and expect it. When we expect something, it is difficult to be thankful for it.

Entitlement makes gratitude impossible.

Gratitude is also a function of attention. I can choose what I want to give my attention to—those things that are going great, or those things that are less than stellar. If I choose to focus on whatever is lacking, or less than stellar, it will be nearly impossible to be thankful.

Why must we practice gratitude?

For exactly the reasons I illustrated earlier. If we don't purposely identify those things that we are grateful for, we will start becoming myopic and self-centered.

What happens when we do practice gratitude?

Exactly what happened to me when I started to really see all the things that I had to be thankful for.

Gratitude has long been extolled by religion and, in recent years, has been given attention through various books.

And thanks to new research, there is scientific evidence that gratitude produces health benefits.

The research is summarized by author and researcher Robert Emmons. Emmons and his colleagues at the University of California at Davis are among the pioneers of gratitude research, part of a larger discipline called positive psychology.

Positive psychology studies health-promoting behavior and the pleasurable parts of life, rather than focusing on illness and emotional problems.

Emmons reports on several studies. In the first, he and his colleagues divided participants into three groups, each of which made weekly entries in a journal. The first group wrote five things they were grateful for. The second group described five daily hassles. And the third group, the control group, listed five events that had affected them in some way.

Here are the results:

Those in the gratitude group felt better about their lives overall, were more optimistic about the future, and reported fewer health problems than the other participants.

Results from a second study suggested that *daily* writing led to an even greater increase in gratitude than just a *weekly* practice.

A third study reproduced the results among a group of people suffering from various neuromuscular diseases, including post-polio syndrome, which has symptoms similar to those of chronic fatigue syndrome (CFS).

Interestingly, the gratitude group also reported getting more sleep, spending less time awake before falling asleep, and feeling more refreshed in the morning.

In a related study, researchers at the University of Connecticut found that gratitude can have a protective effect against heart attacks. Researchers found that heart attack victims who responded positively to their experience—like becoming more appreciative of life—had a lower risk of having another.

This research on gratitude challenges the idea of a "set point" for happiness—a belief that, just as our body has a set point for weight, each person may have a genetically determined level of happiness.

The set point concept is supported by research that shows that people return to a characteristic level of happiness a short time after unusually good and unusually bad events. But the research on gratitude suggests that people can move their set points upward to some degree, enough to have a measurable effect on both their outlook and their health.

So, we have found that those who practice grateful thinking reap emotional, physical, and interpersonal benefits.

People who regularly keep a gratitude journal report fewer illness symptoms, feel better about their lives as a whole, and are more optimistic about the future than those who didn't.

Gratitude is a choice. One possible response out of many to our life experiences.

If you would like to increase the level of gratitude in your life, here are five suggestions that have found to be helpful:

Keep a Daily Gratitude Journal

This is probably the most effective strategy for increasing your level of gratitude. I set aside time—daily—to record three things that I am grateful for. You can write when you get up or at the end of the day. Pick a time that you will consistently have available.

You can buy a journal or use something as simple as loose-leaf paper or a notebook. The important thing is to establish the daily practice of paying attention to gratitude-inspiring events and writing them down. Taking a moment each day to recall those things that I am grateful for increases my awareness of their occurrence in my life.

Use Visual Reminders

Two obstacles to being grateful are forgetfulness and lack of awareness. You can counter them by giving yourself visual cues that trigger thoughts of gratitude.

One suggestion is to put Post-It notes listing your blessings in various places, like your refrigerator, mirrors, and the steering wheel of his car.

I set an alarm on my smartphone to remind me at random times during the day to be thankful. You can use the signal to pause and count blessings.

Recruit a Gratitude Partner

Social support encourages healthy behaviors because we often lack the discipline to do things on our own. Just as you may be more likely to exercise if you have an exercise partner, you may be able to maintain the discipline of gratitude more easily if you have a partner with whom you can share gratitude lists and discuss the effects of gratitude in your life.

If we hang out with ungrateful people, we will "catch" their set of emotions; if we choose to associate with more grateful individuals, the influence will be in another direction. Find a grateful person and spend more time with him or her.

Make a Public Commitment

We feel accountable when we make commitments to others. Create a group that will meet regularly and commit to share your gratitude progress. When a goal is made publicly to a group, we become more likely to follow through.

Change Your Self-Talk

We all carry on an inner dialogue with ourselves that is often called "self-talk." When this inner conversation is negative, our mood is usually low. As I described earlier, research shows that we can change our mood by changing the tone of the things we say to ourselves. (See chapter 5)

Please join me. Let's take a baby step and start with the first of my suggestions. Start keeping a daily gratitude journal. As I described earlier, I have a daily habit of taking time to sit down and quietly consider three things that happened to me that day that I choose to be thankful for. Then I identify one positive experience I had during the day and write that that down too.

This is a practice that I have followed for a while now. I am amazed at the impact it has had on me. I know that you will experience its benefits also.

My goal is to get to a point where I learn that gratitude is not merely dependent on my current life circumstance.

For it is in giving that we receive.

St. Francis of Assisi

A generous person will prosper;

whoever refreshes others will be refreshed.

Jewish Proverb

CHAPTER 10

What Can I Do For You:
The Power of Generosity!

Christmas is my favorite holiday. Man, I love it. Growing up—and I must confess, even now—I found myself putting a pillow under my head as I lay on the floor, my feet shoved under the Christmas tree, and losing myself in the beautiful lights, ornaments, ribbons, and green boughs.

Ebenezer Scrooge sure didn't have the same feeling about Christmas.

Do you remember the story written by Charles Dickens? Ebenezer was going through life being mean-spirited and miserly. He refused to give even a pittance to those in need. Responding with "Bah, humbug!" to every wish of a Merry Christmas!

But then, everything changed with the visitation of Ebenezer's dead partner. The ghost declared that, because of Ebenezer's greedy and self-serving life, his spirit was condemned to wander the earth weighed down with heavy chains.

As the story goes, the ghosts of Christmas past, present, and future, visited Ebenezer. With each visit, he saw life from a different perspective and began to understand that his critical outlook and selfishness were robbing him of life itself.

He awoke and changed his life, spending the rest of his days experiencing the euphoria of generosity.

Remember how you felt when someone was generous to you? Maybe they gave you a thoughtful gift. Maybe they surprised you by mailing you a card. Maybe they babysat for you. Maybe they took you to a special dinner or a simple coffee.

We have all experienced that warm, fuzzy feeling when we receive goodwill from another person. We call it gratitude, which was the topic of the previous chapter.

Did you know that the warm, fuzzy feeling is actually a result of something physiological happening inside of you?

It's the release of something called oxytocin.

Oxytocin is a hormone. It is the hormone that is secreted by a mother during childbirth and nursing. It is sometimes called the "love hormone" because it is also secreted in large doses by a couple during the first six months of their relationship.

Interestingly, oxytocin has been discovered to play a role when a person receives something special from someone special. That feeling of appreciation you feel is actually a physiological response; it is oxytocin being produced in the body.

We even produce oxytocin when we just hear about someone being generous to someone!

And did you know that you can get that same warm, fuzzy feeling when you *give*?

When you are generous, oxytocin is released in your system. The result? The warm fuzzies!

That's what Ebenezer Scrooge experienced, and we can experience it too!

Want to learn more?

If you are like me, you can use all the warm fuzzies that you can get in life.

A good place to start is by defining the term "generosity."

I define generosity as the willingness to give to others something that has value.

To experience the benefits of generosity, we need to understand the word better. Let's do that by breaking down the definition.

First, the attitude is established—the willingness to give.

That attitude is birthed in us when we realize everything that we have to be thankful for. It is amazing how easy it is to be generous when we are grateful and how difficult it is to be generous when we aren't grateful,

When we are grateful, our heart posture will be one of willingness to give.

Giving with a willing heart means that a person has acted without the motivation of guilt or manipulation.

Giving in response to guilt, manipulation, or coercion is not generosity. Interestingly, giving under these conditions does not bring the same physiological benefits.

Also, the fact that someone asks does not always mean that we should give.

For a period of time, I had a weekly breakfast appointment with a local businessman. This man was very well-to-do and also well-liked. Some might wonder if he was well-liked because he was well-to-do. We would talk about the many things of mutual interest: politics, religion, economics, or generosity.

Invariably, at some point in our time together, he would casually remark about a person or persons who had asked him for money.

I would ask, "What did they want money for?" Sometimes the person had a reason for the request; other times he didn't know the reason because he hadn't even asked. Sometimes the purpose for the request was so outlandish that I had to pick up my jaw when I asked if he gave them money and he told me that he had.

He would literally give tens of thousands of dollars away each week—and often it was to people who were just playing on his lack of discernment.

Finally, one day I had had enough. I complimented him on his desire to be generous but explained to him the importance of being wise in his generosity. I suggested that, whenever anyone asked him for money, he first send them to me; they could plead their case to me, and I would take on the responsibility of making sure the need was valid.

He agreed to my suggestion, and we enacted my plan. As you can imagine, there was a huge drop-off in requests because people realized that cash was not going to be so easy to get.

However, some still requested money and were sent to me. I would interview them and investigate their need. Then, at our weekly breakfast, I would tell him which ones I felt were valid based on what I had been able to discover.

At this point, he would tell me which ones he wanted to give to. I would then direct money to the need.

I tell you that as an illustration—it's okay to be discerning in our giving. There are, unfortunately, many who will take advantage of a desire to be generous.

So, we looked at the definition of giving. Let's take a moment and look at the action of giving. I don't mean lending or trading or selling. The whole idea of generosity is giving without expectation of anything in return. No repayment, no special consideration, no quid pro quo—nothing!

We often catch ourselves thinking, *Well, I gave that to him; you think at the very least he would be willing to do this for me.* When we think that, it shows that we didn't really give anything. We traded or bartered it, which is evidenced by the fact that we expected something in return.

Last, let's examine the description of the item given, the "something of value." This could be your time, your ability, or a possession. I call these time, treasure, and talent! It is not considered generosity if you give something away that no longer holds value to you. For example, if the item is obsolete, broken, etc. The requirement of generosity is that the item you give must have value to you.

When I was young, our family served as missionaries in Guatemala. In 1976, Guatemala experienced a horrendous earthquake, which killed over 25,000, injured more than 76,000, and left hundreds of thousands without homes.

Immediately, people jumped into relief efforts, getting medical aid to those had been injured, distributing food, and, later, rebuilding homes, schools, businesses, and churches that had been demolished.

It seemed like we never slept. Every moment was filled with aiding those who were suffering and working to get the country back on its feet. Thankfully, donations began pouring in to assist us.

Someone from the United States had donated an old box truck for us to use in our relief efforts. My father used it to deliver items throughout the country, traversing the treacherous mountain roads with heavy loads.

You will note that I said the truck was "donated." But it is more accurate to say it was "dumped on us." The usefulness of that truck had long passed. Not only was the engine barely able to propel the truck, the tires were bald, and the suspension was spent. If you hit a bump at any speed, the truck would continue bouncing on and on for hundreds of yards.

It was on one of these delivery-relief trips that my father hit a bump just as he was rounding a curve on a narrow strip of road, high in the mountains of Guatemala. The suspension could not cushion the shock, and he went careening off the road. The truck tipped over and slid.

Fortunately, this happened at one of the few places where the road had a shoulder. He did not tumble off the side of the mountain. And he lived to see another day.

But I remember asking myself as a young boy, *What was the truck's previous owner thinking when he sent this deathtrap to us?* Looking back, I would have benefited from understanding the benefits of forgiveness in that point of my life!

Now that we have looked at what generosity is or isn't, let's look at some of the benefits of generosity. Yes, there are benefits to giving, not just to those who are recipients, but to the giver.

Here are some of them:

Generosity minimizes stress.

Would you like a little less stress in you life? Then be generous. Really!

Social psychologist Liz Dunn conducted an experiment where people were each given ten dollars. The recipients were told that they could keep all the money for themselves, or they could give away as much of it as they wanted.

Dunn found that the more money people gave away, the happier they felt. And, conversely, the more money people kept for themselves, the more shame they experienced.

The experiment further discovered that the more shame people felt, the higher their cortisol levels rose. Cortisol is generally understood to increase when a person experiences stress. While some cortisol is good, elevated levels of cortisol leads to increased blood sugar – which can lead to diabetes. It can also lead to weight gain and obesity.

This leads us to the second benefit of being generous:

Generosity makes you healthier and lengthens your lifespan!

Giving of yourself, whether it is time, money, or energy, actually improves your health. Dunn also studied a group of older couples for five years and examined the psychological issues surrounding caring and community.

In all, the study examined over four hundred couples. What researchers found was that those couples who provided tangible forms of help to friends, relatives, and neighbors on average lived longer lives. This, compared with couples who did not help anyone.

Generosity minimizes depression.

The Center for Learning and Occupational Change examined widows to see if giving yielded beneficial results. Results of that study found that widows who were generous, whether with their time, money, acts, or words, were less likely to have their grief develop into depression. Additionally, widows who increased their giving had lower levels of depression in general.

The same results were discovered among dialysis patients. When a patient undergoing dialysis practiced generosity, he or she had lower levels of depressive symptoms over time.

Generosity enhances a person's sense of purpose.

Somehow, when we are generous, we start believing in

ourselves. It somehow seems to justify our existence.

Maybe that is why the Bible says, "It is more blessed to give than to receive."

So, if all this is true, what keeps us from being generous?

I believe that all of us have an innate desire to be generous. For some, it is fully awake. For some, it lies dormant. For others, it occasionally raises its head and makes a noble attempt and then, for a number of reasons, drops below the surface again.

Sometimes our past will keep us from being generous. Maybe someone criticized our earlier attempts, and that wound hasn't healed.

Maybe we've made a mistake in our past, and we feel that precludes us from being helpful now. Friend, we all have skeletons in our closet. Don't let what you have done or what others have done to you keep you from enjoying the beauty of generosity.

Possibly we have the desire to be generous with our abilities, our talents. However, feelings of inadequacy can keep us from being generous, if we feel that our efforts will not be good enough.

Sometimes the belief that we need to have "a lot" in order to give keeps us from giving. Generosity is not defined by the number of zeros in the gift. Similarly, we sometimes feel that we don't have enough for ourselves, so how can we give what we do not have?

I dare you to try.

Using the definition of generosity I provided earlier, step out of your comfort zone and see what happens.

Recently, many wealthy individuals have announced that, upon their deaths, most of their money would go to charity. Huge amounts of money will be donated to legitimate causes.

That is fantastic. But is that really generosity? Is it generosity when you give it away when you know you can't use it anymore?

However, don't let the fact that you don't have much stop you from being generous. Often, we think that we need to be rich to be generous, that our giving is too small to count.

I know of a couple that didn't have millions and yet have impacted tens of thousands of lives because of their generosity.

As a result, this same couple has benefited from the warm fuzzies of generosity more than anyone I know. To this day, I am amazed by their generosity. Throughout their marriage, they continually gave their money, their time, and their abilities in service to others.

Let me illustrate by telling you a story about them. After serving as missionaries, this married pair returned to the United States and discovered that there wasn't much of a job market for retired missionaries.

They scratched and clawed to make a living.

The wife worked in the produce department of the neighborhood grocery store. The husband worked at a upholstering shop and, during harvest, worked marathon hours picking fruit in the orchards of the Pacific Northwest.

That first year back in the United States they made a grand total of $13,000. But they also gave $11,000 away to people and causes that needed it worse than they.

They survived for a year on $2,000!

How do I know?

Because these people are my parents.

Throughout the fifty-eight years of their marriage, they lived a generous lifestyle—always giving.

Just recently, I stumbled upon another person whom my parents had regularly supported financially. This brings to just under a dozen the number of people they assisted regularly up until my father's death. This from a couple who was on a fixed income—and that income didn't include a bunch of zeros.

On top of that, they gave of their time as pastors of the church in their retirement community.

They loved to give.

They loved to give because they had learned to be grateful. Living in an underdeveloped country helps put things into perspective. When many around you only have one change of clothing, no paid vacation, no car, no floor, and no electricity, you quickly realize that you are blessed.

We can only be truly generous when we become aware of how blessed we are. Can I remind you of the topic of chapter 8? Once we are able identify all those things for which we are grateful, then taking the next step of generosity comes naturally.

In my mind, there are actually two types of generosity. The first I call "crisis giving." That's what occurs when we become aware of a need. Maybe it is a natural disaster in Ecuador or a neighbor in need of an emergency medical procedure. The other I call "planned giving." This is when we plan ahead to give. Maybe it is regularly giving money monthly to our church or to a charitable cause.

Every morning at 7:00 a.m., an alarm goes off on my smartphone, reminding me of an appointment I have with myself every day. The reminder simply says, "G3=L!" The letter G stands for *Give*. The 3 stands for *Time*, *Talent* and *Treasure*. The letter L stands for *Live*.

For me, when I am giving of my time, talents, and treasures, I actually come alive. I live.

This daily reminder takes my focus off of myself and whatever good or bad circumstances I am negotiating and puts my sights on how I can bring a little light, a little help, a little life into the lives of others. I call them "Acts of Kindness!"

Then, every night, when I close my day by writing in my journal, I take a moment and reflect on my day and record one of the acts of kindness that I shared with someone that day.

I would love for you to give it a try. I invite you to join me. Don't hesitate. Start giving whatever amount of time, ability, or money that you can. Having said that, I believe that there are times (and things) we should not give.

For example, it would have been better if the truck given to the efforts in Guatemala had been sold as scrap metal. Then the money received from that sale could have gone toward buying a more reliable—and safer—truck.

If you aren't sure of the usefulness of your gift, tell someone about your intention and ask for feedback.

There are times we just simply forget to give. We have the best of intentions, but we have to get the kids to school, go on this business trip, buy the groceries—and before we know it, that good intention is lost in the recesses of our minds.

A solution to this is accountability. Tell someone your plan to give. I suggest this not so someone will think you are incredible but so they will ask you later if you followed through.

Ungratefulness will also keep us from giving. When we are ungrateful, we generally believe we deserve what we have—it's tough to give when you have that attitude.

Let's learn to give for the sheer love of giving, out of gratitude for the many ways we have been blessed. When we do that, we will enjoy the benefits.

Remember, giving doesn't have to be just with dollars. Giving can happen through sharing our abilities or our time with someone.

My challenge to you is each day, for a month, find one totally unexpected kind thing to do for someone— and just do it. Not because of the accolades that you might receive, but just because.

And take notice of what happens in your life.

Exercise is the most under utilized
anti-depressant.

Unknown

CHAPTER 11

Sedentary Malaise:
The Power of Exercise

I have always been a very active person. It was not uncommon for me to get up and be working out at 5:00 in the morning. I loved to exercise. I loved being fit.

I had determined that I was not going to be that 'well-balanced mid-life man'. You know the one with the bubble in the middle. I was not going to let my six-pack become a keg or let my chest fall into my drawers.

Besides that, I loved the exhilaration I felt during and after a good work out.

However, in the middle of my storm, I had gotten to where there were days when it was all I could do to get out of bed – there was no way I was going to exercise, let alone get up at 4:30!

There seemed to be this heavy weight, too large to overcome, pushing me down. At the same time I didn't really want to push it off. I couldn't muster up sufficient mental and emotional energy to care that I wasn't getting out of bed.

If there was some appointment or responsibility that I had to be at, I could muster up the energy and go. Mainly because I knew that if I didn't go questions marks would arise in people's minds. If I didn't show up – people would know that I didn't have it together.

There were days when I wouldn't get out of bed until noon. By 3:00 p.m. I needed a nap and I was ready to call it a day by 8:00 p.m. It seemed the less I did, the less energy I had. The downward spiral was getting the upward hand.

Believe it or not, it was at a church service that I was reminded of the benefits of exercise. It was not the speaker's main point, but he touched just briefly on the topic and encouraged all of us to try to do a minimum of 30 minutes of exercise a day. "Even if all we could manage was a slow stroll," he said "the benefits would be felt."

The reason I found it surprising that exercise was mentioned in church was because for many generations church goers have hid behind the verse in the Bible that says, "Bodily Exercise profits little."

Along with that theological position there was also the fear of offending the attender in the audience who was overweight, or even obese. Growing up I often wondered which came first, the overweight parishioner or the unwillingness to address the value of being fit.

The church background that I come from had quite the list of things that one did not participate in lest you be seen as unholy. But one thing we could do was eat. And because that was acceptable – we had it down to an art form. It seemed that like we were always grabbing a bite together after church, having potlucks, picnics, and fellowshipping over dessert.

You don't have to be a medical expert to know what will happen if you downplay the importance of exercise and yet create multiple opportunities for food and fellowship. You are going to end up collectively gaining weight. How can you preach about the sin of obesity if you as a church are the one who facilitated it?

But it isn't totally the churches fault. We have become such a sedentary society. No longer do we have to walk to the fields and toil sun up to sun down. We don't have to gather wood and cut it for cooking and for heat. We don't have to walk 3 miles to the river for water. We don't have to carry our laundry to the river to wash it by hand.

We sit as we commute to work. We sit for 8 to 10 hours at work. We sit during our lunch break. We sit on our commute home. We sit for dinner. And then in the evenings, because we feel so exhausted we wind down for a few hours of watching television or reading before we turn in for the night.

Often we feel exhausted exactly because we haven't exercised. Let me explain.

When we exercise – however limited it may be – our brain produces endorphins. Endorphines are chemicals that make you feel good and activate the 'happy side' of your brain when produced. Movement causes your brain to produce and release them.

So, when you don't exercise you don't produce endorphins and in turn you feel too exhausted to exercise. That's quite the vicious cycle.

Something stirred inside as I listened to the speaker in that church service. I committed to giving it a go. He encouraged us to do something active for 30 minutes each day. I started, just as he suggested, with just strolling. Soon my pace quickened and the distance I walked lengthened. I began to look forward to these outings. After a bit, I got back on my bike. I would peddle fifteen minutes away from my little apartment and then turn around and peddle back.

Then I began to challenge myself to go further. There was a canal not far from my place and I would set out cycling, exploring, enjoying the sites. There were people fishing, homeless people hanging out, joggers, other bikers. Families of ducks could be found paddling along the banks. Feral cats would dart from bush to bush, evading real and imaginary enemies.

After about six months I began to incorporate more. Planks, weights, yoga, swimming.

After almost a year I progressed so far that I even pretended like I was competing in my own private mini triathlon. I would swim 8 laps, bike 20 miles and then run 3 miles.

Needless to say I experienced first hand the benefit of exercise.

So, how are you doing in the exercise arena?

Did you used to be a jock but now you are out of breath just thinking about it?

Or maybe you never have been into exercise and quite frankly the idea of sweating is detestable to you.

Is the thought of getting out of bed at any hour – let alone at 0 dark thirty too exhausting?

Is there a weight pressing down on you? A darkness? A total lack of energy that won't let you get up and get going?

Are you hiding behind that misapplied Bible verse: 'Physical exercise profits little!'?

Here is a thought. Just start doing something for thirty minutes each day. You could do like I did, just stroll around the block. No one is saying that you need to become a marathon runner or an Olympic. Just move. Just move. Just move.

To keep myself accountable this is something that I write in my journal each day. I have a line that says 'Exercise' and I put down what I did and for how long.

Are there some days when I don't do anything? Yes, but not many. Two things happen: My OCD won't let me leave that line blank and I also am reminded of how good I feel when I have exercised.

Bottom line: Do something! Do something today! Do something every day! Make it a lifestyle, you won't regret it.

Self-compassion is simply giving the same kindness to ourselves that we would give to others.

Christopher Germer

CHAPTER 12

Spoil Yourself:
The Power of Self Care

I grew up in a segment of the population that took great pride in sacrifice and 'going without'. Somehow it was equated to godliness.

It was modeled for me that if there was any excess it should be given away (I confess, I probably still feel this way about excess).

If you have any free time, it should be 'in service to someone or something' – because an idle mind is the Devil's workshop.

Hot water to bathe in was just inside of the acceptable boundaries of luxury. However, one should not spend too much time relishing in that steam induced euphoria.

The evil trap of Hedonism was lurking around every corner!

A vow of poverty was something to be celebrated. If you were rich or were somehow able to accumulate money you would need to watch yourself because, you definitely were a candidate for Satan's temptations! Because we all know "The love of money is the root of all evil."

And in fact, to some degree, your spirituality was measured by how much you could deny yourself. Because you know, we are pretty evil beings.

So, the more you can deny yourself the holier you are!

I used to call myself a machine. I didn't need anything.

I didn't need a break.

I didn't need rest.

I had no feelings.

In this way, I felt that I would be seen as invaluable - some kind of modern living saint.

But is that true? Is that correct?

In Sunday School our attention would be directed to that Bible verse that reads: "Love your neighbor as yourself."

The discussion in our Sunday school class would generally focus on the ways we show people love. This included behaviors like hospitality, manners, patience, and forgiveness.

Rarely do we start with the first step we must take in order to truly love our neighbor like we should: we must first love ourselves.

Hmmm, that feels weird for some of us and can seem hedonistic or just downright wrong.

But you see, how you love your neighbor grows out of how you love yourself.

If you see yourself as a liar, you tend to look for the lies of others.

If you shame yourself for being fat and unattractive, you tend to discredit the beauty of others.

If you see yourself as lazy, you generally have unloving feelings about those who are ambitious.

My motto used to be: "I'd rather burn out than rust out!" This consumed me so much that I actually felt guilty when I relaxed (I must confess I still wrestle with this)!

Which carried over into how much sleep I would allow myself.

You see I thought I needed to prove my value and show that I had what it took to be the go-to-guy'. I even began believing that I was earning God's favor through my tireless efforts, my willingness to go without sleep, making all kinds of sacrifices in the name of service.

I took pride in that I could survive on 4 – 5 hours of sleep a day. I would go to bed late and be up by 4:30 so that I could be at the gym when it opened at 5:00. Yes, I was that guy standing outside waiting for them to open the door!

Surely God would be pleased with me!

In the middle of my Perfect Storm I began to see that maybe, just maybe I was wrong.

Maybe my sacrificing, my self-denial, my abstinence, my austerity, was on one level noble – yet on another level a tad overboard and at the very least not helpful in being a healthy individual.

I stumbled across a study about sleep done in 2015 by Max Hirshkowitz of the National Sleep Foundation. He discovered in his study that:

Infants require about 12-15 hours of sleep a day.

Toddlers require about 11-14 hours of sleep a day.

Pre-School children require 10-13 hours a day.

School-age children require 9-11 hours of sleep a day.

Teenagers need about 8.5-9.5 hours of sleep each day on average.

Most adults need 7-9 hours a night for the best amount of sleep, although some people need as few as 6 hours or as many as 10 hours of sleep each day.

He discovered that if you feel drowsy during the day, even during boring activities, you haven't had enough sleep.

Max went on to talk about what he calls 'Sleep Debt'. "Getting too little sleep creates a "sleep debt," which is much like being overdrawn at a bank. Eventually your body will demand that the debt be repaid."

So, we don't really adapt to getting less sleep than we need. We may get *used* to living on less sleep but our judgment, reaction time, and other functions are still impaired.

The study uncovered the consequences of too little sleep. It found that trying to function on too little sleep is actually not good for you.

Check what the consequences are for lack of sleep:

Memory problems

Depression

A weakening of your immune system

Increase in perception of pain.

Low self-esteem

Feelings of resentment

With that in my mind, I gave myself permission to get more sleep. When I would awake at 4:30, I would roll over and get a few more winks in. I found that a couple times I slept until almost 8:00! Those who know me well, know that is a major act.

Wow, that what a difference letting myself sleep made.

But it was and is really about a lot more than sleep. My philosophy of life was built around the command: "Love others!". A voice in the back of my mind was always saying: "Love others, love others, love others!"

We generally hear the sermon: Love others!

In and of itself, that is not a bad thing. But if taken to extremes it can be incredibly unhealthy.

The command to 'love others' is taken from a larger admonition that actually gives it balance: "Love others.....as you would love yourself!" That makes sense. How can we truly love others if we don't love ourselves?

During my storm I realized that I wasn't doing a very good job of loving myself. Love is proven by how you treat yourself, and by driving myself so hard I definitely was not treating myself in a loving way.

There are many benefits of taking care of yourself. For one, you can prevent chronic stress from damaging your health. It can contribute to long-term feelings of wellbeing.

So, I decided to do a better job of loving myself. I know that not only would it be for my benefit – but I could truly love others once I truly loved myself.

I committed to take better care of myself, and it involved more than just getting more sleep!

Three of the things I began doing, a couple of which men historically shy away from, but I didn't let that stop me.

As my financial situation slowly improved, every three months I scheduled a massage.

Second, I began to regularly schedule a pedicure. Yep you heard correctly. I go to one of those places where you sit in a chair and they soak your fee in hot water and then trim your nails and scrape your callouses off. I will never forget the first time I went they attendant curled up her nose at the sight of the callouses on my feet.

Next, every 6 weeks I would go get my nose, ears and eyebrows waxed. Yup, waxed! I warned you that these fell in the 'Isn't that just for women?' column.

I'm definitely not a hairy gorilla, but I remember when I was young looking at a distant relative and wondering how in the world he could breathe with all of the nose hairs growing out of his nose and how he could hear with all the hairs growing out of his ears and with how bushy his eyebrows were, how could he see?

I also treat myself to at least two rounds of golf each month and on Friday's I buy a bouquet of flowers – for me - to put on my table.

Lastly, I began to spend one day a month by myself in nature. I would go hiking. Or go sit by a seashore. Or something similar

On a spiritual level I began to bathe in the knowledge that God loves me and there was nothing I could do to gain more of his favor, care, protection, adoration and down right pleasure with me.

So, how do you love yourself?

Are you kind to yourself?

Do you say nice things about yourself?

What have you done for yourself lately?

When is the last time you got a massage? Had a long steam shower? A soothing bubble bath? Sat and watched a movie? Took time out for recreational reading? Sat and listened to the waves crash on the shore?

I cannot over emphasize enough the benefit and the necessity of taking care of yourself. If you truly want to love others, you must truly love yourself. Find something that you find enjoyable and refreshing and go do it! You will thank yourself! Others will thank you!

Silence fertilizes the deep place where personality grows. A life with a peaceful center can weather all storms.

Norman Vincent Peale

CHAPTER 13

Button it up:

The Power of Silence

What is it with us and noise?

When I returned to the United States after graduating from High School in Paraguay, I was overwhelmed with all the noise.

No, I'm not talking about the usual lawn mower, a car starting, a cell phone ringing, a toilet flushing.

I'm talking about the absence of silence.

I would ride with my friends to the store to pick up some food and the stereo would be on (loud I might add), we would get out of the car and there would be music playing in the parking lot.

As we entered the store there would be music playing.

As we worked out in the gym, music would be on.

As we at food at a restaurant music would be playing.

As I stood in line at the bank, a television was announcing financial updates and current events.

As I waited at the doctor's office a monitor would be telling me about health issues I needed to be aware of.

It seemed like everywhere I went there was noise. I agree it was usually either beneficial or beautiful noise. I love being well informed and I understand the therapeutic value of music.

But it was everywhere!

Even at church during communion. I mean really, could we have some silence during what many believed to be the most sacred part of the service?

Later, as an adult, my family and I had the privilege of living in the Canary Islands, Spain for a couple of years. The Canary Islands are a popular vacation destination for Europeans.

They would travel to the islands to escape the wet and cold of the northland to enjoy a couple of weeks on the beautiful warm beaches. Each day they would pick their ideal spot in the sand, spread their blankets out, slather on the sunscreen, and as they laid down, would reach over and turn on their radios to enjoy the music from the homeland.

Unfortunately, not everyone likes the same music – even if you are from the same country. And these tourists came from all over Europe. England, Scotland, Ireland, Germany, Holand, Germany, Norway, Sweden, Italy, France were all represented here and of course they all wanted to enjoy a day on the beach, but it couldn't be a quiet one – there had to be music.

You can imagine the resulting cacophony of clashing music styles. Soon the therapeutic sounds of seagulls and crashing waves was a distant memory.

Why are we afraid of silence?

As a consultant, one of my roles is to teach people how to ask for money. Obviously the first step is to actually verbalize the petition. "Mr. Donor would you please consider giving $100,000 to our nonprofit?".

For most that is a big hurdle. Asking for money is not second nature for most and out of nervous worry that possibly we have offended Mr. Donor, we quickly fill the space right after the petition with another statement - anything to avoid the agonizingly awkward moment between the Ask and the Answer.

This is when I teach them the Power of Silence.

The best thing we can do after asking for money is just be silent. Why is that so hard? Why are we allergic to silence?

In my own life, I have always been allergic to silence.

My aural drug of choice was music. If I didn't have it playing, I would provide it – either by whistling a song or singing, or humming.

If I was at someone's house for dinner, if there was a lull in the conversation, I took that as the clarion call for me to step into action and have a quip ready, a question, anything to keep conversation going. Heaven forbid we should have silence!

Why?

Why, when we get home after a long day of listening to people, and a commute home that was spent hearing the latest news updates and current top selling songs, we have the need of turning on the television so that there is noise in the background?

Studies also show the benefits of silence. Dr. Paul Haidier has done studies on the benefits of silence. Here is what he wrote in OMTimes magazine:

There's a lot of great science showing that silence is very beneficial to your health. Noise and especially noise over 30 decibels is associated with high blood pressure, anxiety, and stress. Lots of people get out of bed, take a shower, have coffee and put on the news and starts the cycle of stress for the day.

Silence lowers blood pressure and allows you to deal with life's challenges in a better way.

Silence is like plugging in your phone... your mind needs to recharge too... and it does more recharging in silence than it does during sleep.

Silence is important if it's inside or outside, sometimes you have more chatter going on inside than you have noise outside. Close the door... take a few deep breaths... and sit some where for a while and just watch the chatter slow down.

Silence allows you to find yourself in the midst of all the crazy running around. Especially if you are a busy person, sometimes you get the feeling you are more of a human doing... than a human being... and silence will help you feel human again.

Silence boosts your immune system... making it easier for your body to fight of invading bacteria and other pathogens.

Silence makes you happy, spending time in silence boosts your brain chemistry... and as a great side effect you're able to focus better too!

Silence makes you look and feel younger and at the same time have a lot more energy.

Silence reduces stress (lowers blood cortisol levels and adrenaline levels, which leads to heart disease and is the biggest killer in the world). Adding 30 minutes of silence a day can change your life.

Silence allows for good hormone regulation and interaction of all the hormone related systems in your body.

Silence keeps plaques from forming in arteries... and thus helping to prevent cardiovascular disease and strokes.

Silence reduces pain, and also helps your brain to become more interactive, thus you work with more of your brain... leading to higher cognitive abilities.

I used to be critical those couples I would see in restaurants sitting across from each other at a table and not saying a word. My assessment was that surely their relationship was stale. They were just together because it was easier than going their separate ways.

And, while that may be true for some, I am more inclined to look at that same couple today and say they aren't afraid of silence. They aren't insecure about themselves, nor are they insecure about their relationship. They don't always have to being saying something.

In my own life, I have begun to enjoy the benefits of silence. One of the ways that I have cultivated silence is each morning I sit in meditative quiet for a period of time. I started with 10 minutes and as I experienced its benefits, have increased this moment significantly.

During this time I begin by taking about four big breaths, which help my heart and head to begin to slow down. I close my eyes and allow myself to listen to any sounds that may be present.

I identify the sounds but don't try to imagine or think about what is making them. Then I take inventory of my body. I slowly scan it from head to toe.

I recognize the slight itch in my ear. I identify that there is discomfort in my left shoulder. I recognize that there is a cool breath of air passing by my left calf. I don't try to scratch the itch, nor remedy the discomfort or figure out where the breeze is coming from that is passing my calf.

After that I assess my emotional state. I recognize if I am hopeful, disappointed, anxious, etc.... I don't try to figure out 'why'. I just recognize the fact that I feel that way.

Last I just concentrate on my breath. I don't try to control it or change it. I just breathe in and out in a relaxed manner. As I do, I count 1 as I breathe in, 2 as I breathe out. 3 as I breathe in, 4 as I breathe out.

If a thought comes into my mind other than counting my breath, I try not to engage it - I simply recognize it and let it float away like in a air bubble. And return to counting my breath.

My original goal is to reach 10 without being distracted in thought. Once I reached 10, I would start again at one. If I found myself distracted and that my mind has followed some thought that has entered it. I simply returned to my breath and began counting at 1 again.

I am amazed at the impact this simple exercise has had on me! I can identify with many of the benefits that Dr. Haidier mentions in his article. And my doctor has seen a significant improvement in my blood pressure and other indicators that I attribute to the Power of Silence.

I encourage you to give it a try! Don't be afraid of silence. Listen for its benefits. Listen for its therapy. Listen for God's whisper.

And we know that God causes all things to work together for the good to those who love Him.

Apostle Paul

Chapter 14

Kicking and Screaming:
The Power of Perspective!

As a young boy, I remember attending a community fair. Shortly into the event, I experienced a cakewalk for the very first time. You know what a cakewalk is right? Back 'in the day', it is a game that you could say is a cross between musical chairs and bingo. You purchase a ticket, which gives you the privilege to walk along a path that is marked by numbered squares. As music is played, you walk along the path. Suddenly, the music stops, and a number is called out. If you happen to be standing on the square with that number, you win a cake as a prize.

Seems harmless enough, doesn't it? Well in my young mind, I saw nothing but danger. At this cakewalk, every time they called a number, the person would step behind a draped area and was never seen again.

Where did they go? What happened to them?

There was no way I was going to step onto that path and allow them to call my number. I didn't know that, right behind that curtain, the people were given the opportunity to choose a cake to take home. From my limited perspective, I saw nothing but danger. So, I feared any step that might put me in danger.

I remember kicking and screaming as my parents tried to convince me that it was okay. That it was a good thing. That I might actually benefit if I would just step onto the path.

I felt like I was that little boy again a while back, when a friend of mine invited me to share his house with him.

Let me set this up.

About four months prior to that invitation, due to an inadvertent phone call, my life and the life of my friend had become intertwined.

I was attempting to solve a logistical challenge. I felt that one of two friends could help me with it. In my mind, I clearly made the decision to call one friend but, somehow, found myself telling Siri to call the other. Puzzled, I looked at my phone and wondered why I had done that.

When he answered, I knew why.

He was in trouble.

There is no need to go into the details, but as a result of my friend's predicament, he moved in with me. For four months, we walked through what became an ugly divorce for him.

After living with me for four months, he moved back into his house. But he found himself rattling round a 4,000-square-foot place all by himself. The ominous silence was tormenting him. Memories of family laughter and neighborhood gatherings haunted him.

Hence the invitation to come share the house with him.

Moving in could allow us to continue to walk through this period of life together and simultaneously put a roof over my head.

And not just any roof!

This house has a gourmet kitchen; a pool table; two large flat-screen televisions; a superior sound system, which has speakers inside and out; a crystal-clear swimming pool; and a view of a beautiful golf course. In fact, the community is so beautiful that their tagline is, "Life in Abundance!"

Yet, I hesitated.

Why? Why would I hesitate? Why would anyone hesitate?

Because I saw that invitation just as I saw the invitation participate in that cakewalk so many years ago!

Unfortunately, in that moment, all I could see was my number being drawn and being asked to step behind the curtain where who knows what would happen to me.

His house was smack-dab in the community where my pain started. Where my world fell apart. Where my perfect storm began.

I didn't want to go back; I imagined the worst.

I had made a lot of great memories there, and I had a lot of great friends. But there were moments of great pain, embarrassment, and loss.

A few short months earlier, I had, silently and under the cover of darkness, put my head down, tucked my tail between my legs, and left this community. A community I loved. A community I had called home for sixteen years.

I left broken, disappointed, sad, embarrassed, and alone.

The last place I wanted to return was a place where I had experienced my financial collapse, where there were still people angry about my role in my old church, where there were some who considered me a failure as a father and a husband, and where many still questioned my integrity.

What I feared most was bumping into people and having them confirm what I believed: that everyone thought I was a failure and that everyone hated me.

But return I did.

I accepted my friend's gracious invitation and—literally—returned to the epicenter of my personal storm.

Straight away, a couple of my fears were realized. When I held the door open at a store for the president of the homeowners association, he said thank you by directing a string of four letter words and a look of hatred toward me that shook me to the core.

On another occasion, I greeted a lady who had been a friend of our family, who was seated at a table at the local coffee shop. She responded by gathering her belongings and walking out the door without a word, leaving the friend she was having coffee with alone, her mouth wide-open in surprise.

I would sneak into the grocery store to buy groceries, hoping that I could get in and out without seeing anyone I recognized.

It was on one of those grocery runs that I bumped into a pastor of a church who, I was certain, believed I was a modern day Judas. Let me explain why I say that.

When we as leaders of my church, decided to close its doors, we first reached out to two neighboring churches to see if we could somehow combine forces.

Our church had a fantastic campus. One of those two churches met in a school, which meant they had to set up and tear down every weekend. The other church was leasing space, which left them at the whim of a landlord and the rental market.

The problem was that our monthly mortgage was too high. No one could afford to partner with us.

Well, almost no one.

There was this mega-church, a huge church of 16,000 attendees that wanted to start a campus in our area. They agreed to take on our debt so that we could, as an organization, cease to exist.

Put yourself in the shoes of these two neighboring churches and their pastors. It is kind of like what happens to the mom-and-pop stores when a big box store moves into town; these small churches and their pastors are functioning on a limited budget, making every dollar stretch as far as possible, and along comes this church with seemingly unlimited resources, which allows them to offer unlimited programing, ministries, and marketing. How could they compete?

So, fast-forward to the canned-good aisle at the grocery store. I'm now face-to-face with one of those local pastors, whom I had not seen or talked to since we had made the decision to go with the mega-church.

I couldn't avoid him—he blocked the aisle. I said, "Hello," in a sheepish, guilty way.

He replied, "Hello."

I so wanted to bolt but couldn't. I was positive he was going to unleash a lecture—not because he was of that nature, but because I was certain that I knew how he felt about the decision we had made.

Instead, to my surprise, he embraced me with words of acceptance and affirmation. He told me that he desperately wanted to reconnect and that it had been "too long."

I went home and enjoyed the warm healing that had just occurred.

Around this same time, I visited a church where a friend of mine often played the drums in the worship band. I didn't want to go, but he had invited me, and I really wanted to see him "in action."

My hope was to get in and out without anyone noticing me; this was the other neighboring church our leadership had conversed with when we had been trying to dissolve. I felt certain the pastor cursed the day of my birth.

To my horror, I practically ran into the pastor as I walked through the door. I couldn't avoid him. I hesitantly reached out my hand to greet him, and he said, "Are you kidding me? A handshake?"

My heart stopped.

Surely he wasn't going to make a scene right here in front of everyone.

"A hug is what I want to give you," the pastor said, and he drew me into one of those warm, hearty, bear hug embraces.

My heart melted at this expression of love.

Not long after that, I had coffee with both of these pastors. Accompanying the coffee was an incredibly affirming, healing conversation.

A huge lesson that I began to learn was, your perspective can make all the difference.

I had a skewed perspective and had seen the invitation to move back to the geographical epicenter of my perfect storm to be just like that first cakewalk. Stepping onto the numbered path would just put me that much closer to the ominous curtain, where, surely there was only pain and suffering. When really, by stepping into the cakewalk, I would be placing myself in a position to receive a beautiful treat.

Likewise, by changing my perspective, I saw that when I accepted the invitation to move back to my hometown, I positioned myself to receive the greatest treat that I could have dreamed of at that time: the treat of restored friendships.

Is my perfect storm over? Yes, it is. There are still waves that seem threatening. But I have a different perspective now. So my attitude is different.

Instead of whining, "why me?" when something less-than-desirable happens, I am learning to look at circumstances differently.

As life unfolds each day, I try to immediately filter my response. If, for some reason, I have negative feelings about something that occurs or develops, I ask myself, *why?* Generally, it is because I expected something else.

I invite you to give it a try. The next time you are confronted with a situation that disappoints you or is different from what you had hoped try these tips:

- Look at the circumstance from a different perspective. See the circumstance as if you never really expected anything in the first place—good or bad.

- Instead of judging a circumstance as being "bad," merely define it as a circumstance.

- Instead of responding with a negative emotion, take a moment to be introspective. Ask yourself if the circumstance is actually bad or if you are looking at it through a lens of expectation.

My perspective is back to where it should be.

My meaning—my purpose—is larger than what I do, what I have, and whom I know, and therefore it cannot be sunk by a couple of rogue waves.

It was a long, tough storm, but I have come out the other side stronger, healthier, and more mature.

My hope is that my story and my struggle can bring you hope, comfort, encouragement, and insight on how you too can overcome your perfect storm.

The phoenix must burn to emerge.

Janet Fitch

CHAPTER 15

Smooth Sailing:
The Power of Affirmation

I left town again!

Only this time, I left differently. A friend planned a going-away party for me, and it was more than I could have ever hoped. A group of friends and I gathered for an evening of reminiscing and reconnecting. After a couple of hours, about a dozen or so of those of us who remained wandered outside and sat around the fire pit. We shared laughs and memories, and we basked in that wonderful moment of being in the presence of people who know and accept you—where there is no need to perform or pretend.

We took turns telling stories about how we had met each other. It was fun to hear the serendipitous stories of how we were all connected.

A friend spoke up. "Let's go around the group and tell Doug how he has impacted us."

As each person shared a memory, the long list of affirmations blew my mind. They spoke to the deepest part of me.

I was embraced by their kind words of how I had, in one way or another, been a positive part of their lives. A sense of worth, value, and purpose flooded my heart, and I knew that indeed I would survive this storm and any other that came my way.

When my dear friends were finished speaking, I told each one what they meant to me.

Too soon, the evening was over, but then, moments like these don't last forever.

It might not feel like it, but neither does the perfect storm.

You will learn that as you implement the truths that are outlined in this book, the storms don't seem as daunting. You will find that you have the skills, the resources to navigate the wind and the waves.

I would love to help you implement these truths. Maybe I can help you find a Very Inspirational Person for your life. Reach out to me! My email address is

Doug@giveservelive.com.

In the meantime, here is a tool for you to help put into practice the truths that were presented in the chapters you just read. I use it every day and that I think would be very useful to you.

Choose a time each day where you can sit uninterrupted and in silence for a few moments and consider what has transpired in your life in the previous 24 hours. I find that evenings just before I go to bed are the most beneficial for me.

First, write down three things that you are thankful for. Next, write one Positive Experience that happened to you today. Next, record one Word of Affirmation that you spoke to someone today, and then record one Act of Kindness that you extended today.

After that, record the moments spent meditating (10,20 30 minutes, or more). And last write down what exercise you did each day and for how long.

168

Author Biography

As a native of Arizona, I am a self-described desert rat. When I was ten, our family moved to Latin America, where we served as missionaries.

It is my parents who first instilled in me the desire to live my life in service to God and to others. As a result, I have had the opportunity to rub shoulders with people in over fifty countries and almost every state in the United States.

These life experiences have forever impacted me, and I consider myself a truly rich person – both because of the many friendships around the work and the amazing opportunities they have provided.

If you think your group would benefit from my sharing the truths found in this book in a live context. Please feel free to reach out to me. I am comfortable and have been well received in both 'secular' and 'religious' settings.

Doug@DCGX3L.com

www.ingramcontent.com/pod-product-compliance
Lightning Source LLC
LaVergne TN
LVHW051409080426
835508LV00022B/3000